PLAYING THE VIOLIN

PLAYING THE VIOLIN

AN ILLUSTRATED GUIDE

Mark Rush

Photography by Dana Duke

Routledge
Taylor & Francis Group
New York   London

Routledge is an imprint of the
Taylor & Francis Group, an informa business

Published in 2006 by
Routledge
Taylor & Francis Group
270 Madison Avenue
New York, NY 10016

Published in Great Britain by
Routledge
Taylor & Francis Group
2 Park Square
Milton Park, Abingdon
Oxon OX14 4RN

Printed in the United States of America on acid-free paper
10 9 8 7 6 5 4 3 2 1

International Standard Book Number-10: 0-415-97886-6 (Softcover)
International Standard Book Number-13: 978-0-415-97886-6 (Softcover)
Library of Congress Card Number 2005032851

Library of Congress Cataloging-in-Publication Data

Rush, Mark, violinist.
  Playing the violin : an illustrated guide / Mark Rush ; photography by Dana Duke.
    p. cm.
  Includes bibliographical references and index.
  ISBN 0-415-97885-8 (hb) -- ISBN 0-415-97886-6 (pb)
  1. Violin--Instruction and study. 2. Violin-- Performance. I. Duke, Dana. II. Title.

MT260.R87 2006
787.2'193--dc22   2005032851

Taylor & Francis Group is the Academic Division of Informa plc.

Visit the Taylor & Francis Web site at
http://www.taylorandfrancis.com

and the Routledge Web site at
http://www.routledge-ny.com

Table of Contents

Acknowledgments

Before writing this book, I often viewed long lists of names on the acknowledgments page of books as being somewhat excessive. Now, I know otherwise. In completing this project, so many people have given kind and valuable assistance — some I've never personally met, while others are close friends and family members.

Since the visual images were considered equal to the text from the outset, I first wish to thank Dana Duke, whose skill and professionalism were a marvel and inspiration. I especially appreciated his extreme cool when disaster struck on the first day of shooting.

A very special thanks goes to the models for this project, Alex Woods and my dear daughter, Sophie Gibson-Rush. Their patience, humor, and sustained concentration streamlined the photo shoot.

I'm indebted to my close friend and colleague Patrick Neher, who saved me when it was discovered that several key photos were missing. He deftly was able to approximate the look of Dana's work and produced the needed images. His photos are duly noted.

A word of thanks to Gary Cook and Ryan Huxtable. Both offered invaluable advice early on that greatly facilitated the completion of the project.

Susan Kempter and my sister, Celeste Rush, must be mentioned here. Both read the manuscript at various stages and offered insightful suggestions pertaining to the content, clarity, and syntax of the book.

Finding a title proved to be difficult — that is, until Delia and Roy Tedoff got involved in a brainstorming session. For this and their wonderful hospitality, a warm thank you is extended.

Others who have given me assistance at some point include Lindsey Robb, Ingvi Kallen, Lisa Olsen Stewart, Michal Venera, and Rodney Yee.

Finally, I wish to acknowledge my spouse, Tannis Gibson, though words cannot express my deep appreciation for all her support. Balancing family and career is always a challenge, and on this score Tannis made it possible for me to find the time and space necessary to complete this project. As my trusted partner and most reliable critic, I have come to depend on her observations and suggestions, which are invariably on the mark and always reflect the pursuit of excellence.

Introduction

A common conception regarding learning to play the violin is that it is the most difficult of all instruments to master. It's true, violin playing *is* difficult, but it becomes much less so when the basic setup is well established. *Setup* refers to the basic physical elements of violin playing — how one holds the violin and bow, one's posture and position, basic movements left and right, and so forth. These are the fundamental components necessary for success. The earlier these concepts are established, the better. Of course, getting things right from the very start is the best approach of all. Because the body readily remembers first sensations when doing something new, those first sensations are crucial, as they easily become future habits or tendencies.

Unfortunately, problems with the setup are all too prevalent. As a teacher of violin at the university level, I confront this problem yearly. At audition time each spring, I often meet talented students who are limited by a poor physical approach to the instrument. The college years are a time when students should be devoting themselves to learning repertoire. It is pointless to do so if the basic setup is amiss. In some cases, it can take a year or two to get the basics in order, a task complicated by the fact that older students lose some of the physical malleability that comes naturally for children.

Teaching the violin setup should be the primary concern for teachers before all else. Students, too, need to explore the physical elements of violin playing in an effort to maximize comfort and freedom. The singular goal of this book is to help clarify the specific components that constitute a good setup.

The material in this book differs from string methods intended for children. Although many ideas certainly overlap, teaching children necessarily takes into account a different set of expectations and parameters than those one applies to an adolescent or an adult. Children tend to *grow* into the violin. With good guidance they evolve over many years into accomplished players.

In this book, the violin setup is a fully realized construction, in other words, the finished product, or the "adult" realization.

Teaching the violin setup also should be distinguished from specific string techniques, such as bow strokes, shifting, fingering, and the development of the left hand — skills Carl Flesch defines as *applied technique*. Instead, the violin setup refers to the *form* of playing. It is the base upon which technique develops.

As a violin student myself, I was fortunate to have a teacher early on (Leonard Felberg of the University of New Mexico) who emphasized the physical aspects of playing. Later, I worked with many of the finest artist–teachers of the twentieth century, including Ivan Galamian, Dorothy DeLay, Szymon Goldberg, and Arthur Grumiaux. Through these experiences, I learned that the principles of violin playing are actually quite universal. Though differences of opinion do exist between teachers, often it is *how* an idea is expressed rather than the fundamental principle that differs. I have noticed that the best violinists tend to do many of the same things. More than anything else, the variation of physiques accounts for differences between players, rather than the actual approach. (The one exception to this is in regard to the bow grip.)

It is often remarked that the best way to learn something well is to teach it. In my case, years of teaching have helped me distill the basics of violin playing into a system that I believe is both simple and easy to understand. The concepts that define a good violin setup are not difficult to grasp. They can be readily understood by anyone. One will spend long hours training the body to master certain skills, but the conceptual idea behind those skills need not be obtuse.

This idea was made especially clear to me after I spoke at national conventions for both the American String Teachers Association and the Music Teachers National Association. My presentation at both events addressed teaching the violin setup. I expected to be speaking to a small number of studio teachers but instead found myself in front of a large, diverse audience. It quickly became clear that some in attendance were not string players at all but had been placed in positions (usually as orchestra directors) in which they needed practical information regarding string playing. In fielding a barrage of questions after my presentation, I recognized the need for source material about violin playing that was accessible to a wide audience.

Many excellent books about violin playing already exist. The problem with many of the classic texts on the subject is that they were written for "insiders," or people already "in the know." These books tend to be text-dense and minimally illustrated, rendering them mostly inaccessible to people who have not previously encountered the central ideas. Even for students with years of experience, the traditional texts can seem remote.

Serious violinists will continue to "tweak" the setup throughout their playing career. They will try this shoulder pad or that one, or perhaps try not using one at all. They might experiment with the position of the left thumb to see how it might affect the vibrato. To experiment in this way is healthy. Teachers need to do much the same thing with their students. Taking time to work with issues relating to the setup in every lesson is time well spent. Most important, teachers should insist on students "getting it right," not giving up until a skill is mastered. Working with a particular concept, say contact point, might require an effort lasting months. Teachers who allow things to slip by are, in the end, doing their students a grave disservice.

For the advanced player, the violin setup must past the ultimate test — performance. I know for myself that performances have taught me the most valuable lessons. When we perform, all is revealed. One might notice the left hand getting tight during a concert, or perhaps that a well-practiced difficult passage seems suddenly impossible to play. Perhaps the hands get strangely cold during the performance. All these issues could be related to the setup. The left thumb might be clenching the side of the neck, or the fingers could be applying too much force rather than releasing. Poor posture might be creating a constriction somewhere in the body. Whatever the case, shortcomings are accentuated when we perform. When we encounter them, it is good to evaluate the basics. As my teacher Szymon Goldberg once said, "The better we play, the more we need to work on the basics."

I have endeavored to present the material in a systematic way and as succinctly as possible in the hope that this book will be as relevant to students and teachers in the studio as it might be for music teachers in the schools. The book is constructed so that each chapter builds upon the last until the violin setup is fully realized. One can read the book from beginning to end, preferably with the instrument close at hand, which will give a comprehensive view of the material, or one might refer to individual sections as needed.

As mentioned previously, I have intentionally omitted issues related to the development of technique or specific musical concerns, which I feel belong in another volume. While I fully realize there might be some differences of opinion regarding certain points, apparent differences are often semantic. In fact, there is considerable latitude, or variations on a theme, when it comes to playing the violin, as long as fundamental principles provide the structure. These principles, I hope, will be amply clear to every reader.

1

The Elements of Good Posture

The key to an optimal violin setup lies in establishing a good basic posture. All physical disciplines emphasize posture as an essential building block. Violin playing is no different, yet paradoxically even holding the violin tends to encourage terrible postural deformations. Let's acknowledge from the start that playing the violin is *not* particularly natural or comfortable. It takes much practice and physical conditioning to finally feel at home with the instrument. Even then, most violinists continue to "tinker" with the violin setup throughout their lives in an effort to find greater ease, comfort, and efficiency.

For any player, poor posture eventually becomes an enormous handicap. By applying a few basic principles, however, we can go a long way toward eliminating bad tendencies. Let's start by taking a look at the spine itself.

THE SPINE

Understanding the basic shape of the spine is critical to establishing good posture, and not just for violin playing! Notice the backward S shape of the spinal column. Our spines naturally curve forward in the cervical and lumbar regions and backward in the thoracic area.

Maintaining these curves in the spine is a question of alignment — ears in line with shoulders, shoulders over hips, and hips over knees and feet. Unfortunately, daily life tends to conspire against our best efforts to establish good posture. Sitting at computers, in car seats, and in most furniture encourages us to slouch and slump.

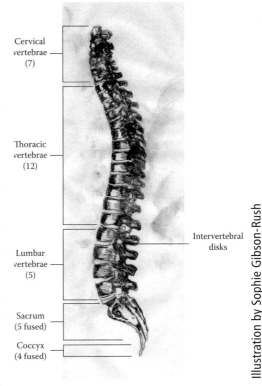

Cervical vertebrae (7)

Thoracic vertebrae (12)

Lumbar vertebrae (5)

Intervertebral disks

Sacrum (5 fused)

Coccyx (4 fused)

Illustration by Sophie Gibson-Rush

POSTURE

All physical disciplines, whether in sports or the arts, emphasize the importance of good postural principles. In yoga, to name but one example, posture and body alignment is a critical element. Great attention to alignment is required to perform a yoga asana well.

In the yoga sitting pose, perfect alignment can be observed — ears over shoulders, shoulders over hips, chest open with the shoulder blades slightly descending into the back. The natural curvature of the back is optimal.

For violinists, attention to good posture is the important first step toward a successful violin setup.

Photo by Michael Venera

THE STANDING POSITION

The photographs demonstrate good principles of posture. Again, notice the alignment of the ears, shoulders, hips, knees, and feet. The feet are directly under the hips and shoulders. The chest is open and lifting.

 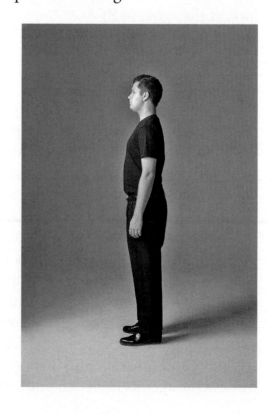

Poor posture tends to fall into two categories: *kyphosis* — the upper back is rounded and the head thrust forward (*slumping*), and *lordosis* — the lower back is curved inward excessively (*sway-back*). Locked knees often accompany *swayback* posture.

In this example of kyphosis, or slumping, the shoulders are rounded, the head held forward, and the chest collapsed. Don't do this.

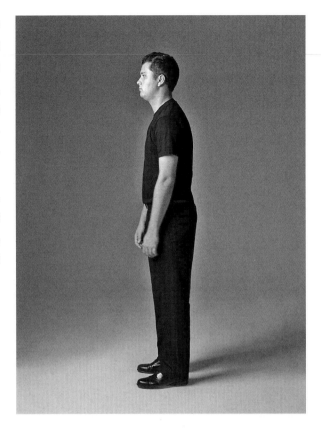

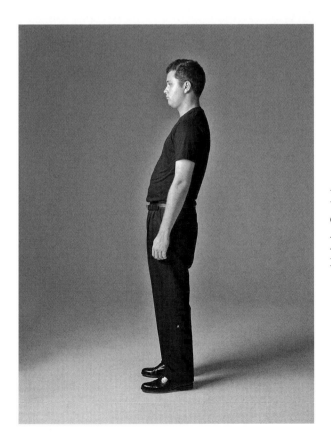

Here is an extreme example of lordosis, or swayback. Notice that the proper alignment discussed above is distorted. Don't do this either.

Here, the student is standing sway-backed, with shoulders rounded and head forward.

Here, the posture is corrected.

THE SITTING POSITION

It is equally important to apply the principles of good posture to the sitting position since violinists do a great deal of playing in a chair.

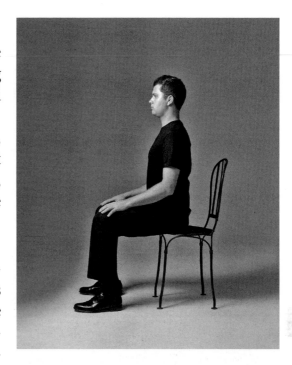

Notice the line of the ears, shoulders, and hips. The chest is open and the feet are under the knees. In violin playing, it is important to sit at the *edge* of the chair.

Now look at the next two photographs. Look familiar? These examples illustrate tendencies to avoid. In the first, the model sits swaybacked (lordosis), and in the second, he sits slumping (kyphosis), a common position for people at the computer.

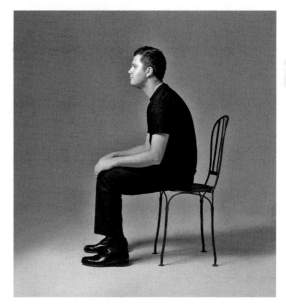

THE ARMS

For a violinist, good posture includes the feeling of suspended arms. Unfortunately, this is not a particularly natural thing to do. It takes years, in fact, for a violinist to develop the muscles to the point at which holding the arms aloft becomes comfortable. When we play, the deltoid muscles in both arms must work to suspend the arms. For less experienced players, this usually represents a major hurdle to overcome and will initially cause some discomfort. It is very important to avoid raising the shoulders while holding the arms aloft.

These photographs illustrate front and side views of good posture, both sitting and standing, with the arms suspended.

CONCLUSION

Developing good postural habits means greater ease of playing. When the body alignment is poor, the muscles we use to play work in opposition to one another. Of course, this translates into tension for the player. In Chapter 5, the issue of good posture is examined once again, with the violin in position. For now, let's turn our attention to holding the violin.

2

Holding the Violin

The way we hold the violin provides the crucial cornerstone upon which all violin technique rests. Problems with the violin position negatively affect every facet of violin playing. The optimal violin position is directed to one primary goal: *It should maximize freedom of movement and minimize the amount of tension.*

BASIC GUIDELINES FOR HOLDING THE VIOLIN

Of course, there are a variety of ways to achieve an optimal violin position, but despite differences of approach, nearly all methods have basic principles in common. These can be distilled into a few simple guidelines, as follows:

THE VIOLIN IS …

- Held parallel to the floor.
- Placed on the collarbone.
- Held at approximately a 45° angle to the horizontal line of the body.
- Held by three points of contact: The placement on the collarbone, in the left hand, and by the weight of the head on the chinrest.

> **Note:**
>
> For those readers completely unfamiliar with the basics of violin playing, "parallel to the floor" refers to the general line of the violin in relation to the line of the floor. It does not mean that the back of the instrument is parallel to the floor. Another way to think of it is to keep the line of the strings parallel to the floor. The phrase "45° angle to the line of the body" refers to the general line of the violin as it relates to the horizontal line of the shoulders.

HOLDING THE VIOLIN IN SIX EASY STEPS

1. *Hold the left arm in front of you, parallel to the floor, palm facing up, fingers and thumb straightened. Try to maintain good posture, head in line with the shoulders, shoulders slightly rolled back and chest open, slightly lifting.*

2. *Bend the arm at the elbow so that a 90° angle is formed at the elbow joint. The fingers remain pointed upward and the thumb is held close to the hand, bent slightly outward, forming a V.*

3. *Rotate the forearm slightly to the left. Maintain the finger position.*

4. *With the right hand, find the hollow above the collarbone. This is where the violin will rest.*

5. *Fit the violin into the position. Notice that the violin is held parallel to the floor and is placed at a 45° angle to the line of the body. The head is held in a neutral position, and good posture is maintained.*

6. *Finally, the chin is lowered to meet the chinrest. Try not to turn or twist the head. Keep it aligned with the vertical center of the body.*

Now, we must decide what to do with the space existing between the back of the violin and the shoulder. How we handle this space is an important concern for every violinist. Do we raise the left shoulder to meet the back of the violin? Do we hold the violin more in the left hand and keep the shoulder relaxed? Or do we fill the space with a shoulder pad? This decision will fundamentally change the way we play the violin. It is a controversial issue, with advocates for each approach.

THE SHOULDER PAD, OR NOT ...

Whether or not to use a shoulder pad is an important question for aspiring violinists. Many concert violinists do not use a shoulder pad at all. Some put padding under their clothing. Still others play with modern shoulder pads. Some teachers insist their students play without a pad; others believe the shoulder pad is a necessity. In between are as many variations as can be imagined.

Violinists who don't ...	Violinists who do ...
Itzhak Perlman	Pinchas Zuckerman (pad under clothing)
Jascha Heifetz	Isaac Stern (pad under clothing)
Aaron Rosand	Arthur Grumiaux (shoulder pad)
Anne-Sophie Mutter	Joshua Bell (shoulder pad)
Leila Josefowicz	Gidon Kremer (shoulder pad)
Nathan Milstein	Gil Shaham (shoulder pad)
Jamie Laredo	Maxim Vengerov (shoulder pad)
Michael Rabin	Midori (shoulder pad)
Zino Francescatti	Sarah Chang (shoulder pad)
Henryk Szeryng	Nadia Salerno-Sonenberg (shoulder pad)

There is a fundamental difference in technique between violinists who use a shoulder pad and those who do not. Any optimal violin position is a question of balance. Remember, the violin rests on the collarbone, in the left hand, and is weighted by the head. The major difference between those who use a pad and those who do not is the degree to which the violin is held in the left hand.

Violinists trained to play without a shoulder pad learn to hold the violin *more* in the left hand. Those who play with a shoulder pad tend to rely on the support of the pad and the weight of the head to hold the instrument. The difference between the two approaches is most vivid when we shift. Without a shoulder pad, one learns to shift while still supporting the instrument in the left hand. When playing with a shoulder pad, the weight of the head and the support of the pad *release* the left hand for the shift.

Clearly, either method can be successful, and in my view it is a mistake to be dogmatic about whether or not a student uses a shoulder pad. As a general observation, however, those who do not use a shoulder pad usually have played that way from early on. It is *very* difficult for a violinist who has used a pad for many years to play without one.

In my own case, I have used some sort of shoulder pad all my life and find playing the violin without one virtually impossible. Therefore, I will leave it for others to explain the best way to play without a shoulder pad and proceed with how one successfully chooses an appropriate pad.

HOW TO CHOOSE AND FIT A SHOULDER PAD

If a shoulder pad is used, it is critical to fit it properly. A poorly fitted pad makes an optimal setup difficult to achieve. Given the vast choice of shoulder pads available on the market today, how do we choose the right one? Here are a few guidelines:

A SHOULDER PAD SHOULD …

- Not lift the violin off the collarbone.
- Fill the space between the back of the violin and the shoulder without the player having to raise the shoulder and/or distort the posture.
- Allow for some lateral movement in the violin position.
- Provide firm support.

As a general observation, not enough time is spent selecting the right shoulder pad. Many teachers routinely suggest the same pad for all their students. In fact, shoulder pads vary widely and must be carefully tailored to each physique.

Furthermore, as a young violinist grows, at some point the shoulder pad may no longer fit. Teachers have an important responsibility to watch for this and to help find an appropriate solution.

> **Note:**
>
> Anytime we change the shoulder pad or chinrest, it will feel strange, perhaps even uncomfortable. We always gravitate toward what feels familiar, even when it is not in our best interest. When searching for the right shoulder pad or chinrest, visually analyze the way it fits by following the guidelines above. How the shoulder pad "feels" initially is not a good means of evaluation.

AVOID THESE PITFALLS

One common mistake is for a violinist to choose a shoulder pad that is too high. This is easily recognized, because the violin no longer rests on the collarbone.

Although a high shoulder pad might seem to give good support, in actuality it makes it more difficult to hold the violin parallel to the floor. Typically, a shoulder pad that is too high will result in the violin slanting toward the floor.

When the shoulder pad is too high, a violinist must raise the left arm higher than necessary to keep the violin parallel to the floor. This is uncomfortable, causes muscular fatigue (which is why the player tends to allow the instrument to slant downward), and can cause chronic tension in the muscles between the shoulder blades, which are constantly having to lift.

Shoulder pads that set the violin into one place, eliminating the possibility of any lateral movement, can be a problem for some players. Shoulder pads of this type often have a pronounced curvature

Here the shoulder pad is too high and tends to lift the violin off the collarbone

The violin slants toward the floor. Remember, holding the instrument parallel to the floor is optimal

designed to fit over the shoulder. Whereas this type of pad might fit one player perfectly well, it might cause another to hold the violin in a position inappropriate for his or her individual physique. The ability to move the violin laterally is generally a positive thing, and in some cases it is crucial to the overall setup, as we will discuss in a later chapter.

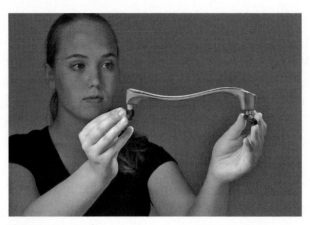

The Kun type pad

Sometimes a shoulder pad provides insufficient support. Usually this is because the pad contacts the body in one place but leaves gaps elsewhere. Simply adjusting the pad might solve the problem, but it could also be that the pad is inappropriate for the player and something different is required.

Example of poor contact with the body ...   ... now properly fit

Remember, the shoulder pad should provide firm support. This is best accomplished when the space between the back of the violin and the body is taken up fully by the pad.

Finally, shoulder pads that are "cushy" or "springy" should be avoided, as they do not provide enough necessary support. Because these pads "give," they increase the tendency for the player unknowingly to squeeze the instrument with the shoulder and head. Any appropriate shoulder pad should approximate the same firmness felt when playing the instrument without a pad but at the same time eliminate any tendency to raise the shoulder.

THE CHINREST

Equally important to the setup is the chinrest. The chinrest and the shoulder pad work together; the choice of one will necessarily affect that of the other. Often, students will use whatever chinrest comes with the instrument. This is a mistake. As with shoulder pads, there is an enormous variety of chinrests on the market, which can accommodate nearly every sort of physique. Basic guidelines for selecting a chinrest include the following:

THE CHINREST SHOULD …

- Fit just under the jawbone. The chin itself will tend to fall onto the tailpiece (or close to it).

- Be of sufficient height. The head should not have to be lowered excessively to meet the chinrest.

- Not distort the elemental posture. The head or neck should not turn or twist to accommodate the chinrest.

- Not cause irritation (the famous neck mark).

A FEW POINTERS

As a general rule, a student with a long neck requires a higher chinrest. Many models come in varying heights. Chinrests with sharp edges are often the culprit for marks on the neck. Chinrests with rounded edges and cups of different depths can alleviate this problem. Also remember, any wooden chinrest can be sanded to make it more comfortable. Most good luthier shops will be happy to help customers in this regard. Some will even make custom chinrests. Be careful about chinrests that fit over the tailpiece in the center of the instrument ("Flesch" model). This type of chinrest can work for some violinists, but for others it results in a badly distorted posture.

Holding the violin well results in freedom of movement and reduces tension for a player. As an added bonus, a good position increases the sound quality and projection of the instrument. Simply raising the violin from a slanting position to one in which it is held parallel to the floor has an immediate effect on the sound. Conversely, a poor violin position can produce chronic tension for a violinist and has a dampening effect on the sound. The greater the ease of playing, the better the sound.

A good violin position is a matter of the shoulder pad, the chinrest, and the placement of the instrument working together to maximize physical freedom and comfort. Don't be afraid to take the time necessary to get things right. By keeping in mind the basic principles outlined above, and through careful analysis and much experimentation, it is possible to find your optimal setup.

In Chapter 5, we will further examine the position of violin as it relates to drawing the bow. For now, however, let's turn our attention to the left hand and arm.

3

THE LEFT HAND AND ARM

The principles of a good violin position discussed in the previous chapter relate very closely to the development of left hand technique. Only when the violin is held properly will the left hand and arm have the necessary freedom of movement. An optimal left hand and arm position will maximize ease, efficiency, and consistency of movement. The left hand and arm must feel "structured," with clear lines and forms defined in the musculature. Teachers call this basic structuring of the left hand and arm the *hand frame* or *hand block*. Mastering this essential aspect of technique will greatly improve one's intonation, dexterity, shifting, and vibrato.

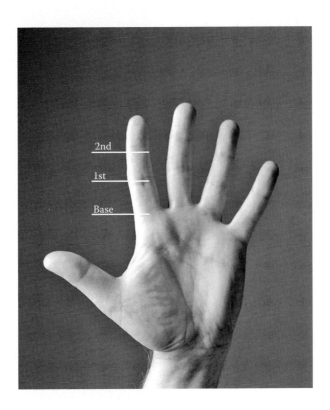

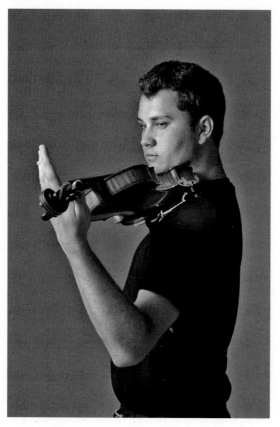

Let's return to the basic violin position established in Chapter 2. Notice that when the fingers are held at attention, as though reaching upward, a V is formed between the thumb and the index finger. The neck of the violin rests in this V and should touch the side of the index finger at the base joint and the thumb at the first joint.

ESTABLISHING THE THREE POINTS OF CONTACT

Three points of contact are maintained between the violin and the hand at all times. In the lower positions, these points of contact are with the thumb, the side of the index finger, and the fingertip on the string.

1. *The neck of the instrument will contact the base joint of the index finger.*

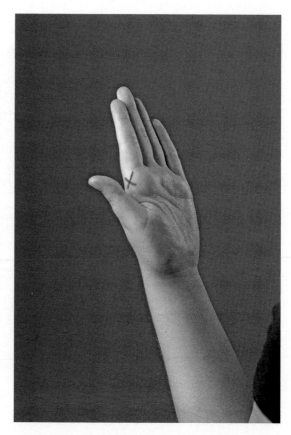

2. *The neck will contact the thumb right on top of the first joint.*

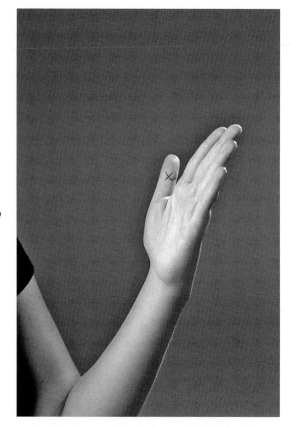

3. *As the fingers are brought to the string, the completed position is established.*

Note:

As we shift to the higher positions, the base joint of the index finger leaves the neck of the violin. As it does so, the heel of the hand touches the shoulder of the instrument, replacing the index finger as the point of contact. Three points of contact are still maintained, regardless of the position.

THE THUMB

The thumb position is critical. It should support holding the violin while also providing counter-pressure to the fingers on the string. It is best to place the thumb *opposite the index finger.* (For students with smaller hands, moving the thumb toward the second finger can be helpful.)

Maintain the basic V shape defined by the thumb and the index finger. The V shape keeps the thumb from gripping the neck of the instrument. It is important not to squeeze the thumb and index finger together. Keep the base joint of the thumb soft. Finally, make sure the neck of the violin contacts the thumb at the first joint.

Here are two views of the thumb position. Notice how the neck of the violin rests in the V formed by the thumb and the index finger.

AVOID THESE PITFALLS

1. *Gripping the neck with the thumb should be avoided. Doing so creates obvious tension and restricts the free and fluid movement of the hand.*

2. *Another frequent problem is placing the thumb too far under the neck of the instrument. This tends to distort the shape of the hand position and also prevents the thumb from offering sufficient support for the finger pressure.*

3. *Some violinists play with a high
    thumb, which I cannot advo-
    cate. A high thumb prevents
    the thumb from providing
    counter-pressure to the fingers
    and encourages a player to grip
    the neck. Furthermore, when
    one shifts, an extra movement
    is necessary, as the thumb must
    drop back before the shift to a
    higher position is executed.*

When the thumb position is correct, the entire hand moves as a unit, as if upon a rail (the violin neck), forward and back through the first three positions while not significantly changing shape. If the neck of the instrument is resting on the first joint of the thumb, as described above, the thumb should be in its proper position.

Finally, the position of the thumb can greatly improve the finger action, shifting, and especially the vibrato, all of which we will explore in more detail later.

Note:

For an advanced violinist, the thumb is not truly fixed. In fact, the thumb must change position frequently. Think of the thumb position described above as a *base position*.

THE WRIST

The position of the wrist is another important aspect of the left hand setup. When the wrist is in its proper position, a line is formed from the index finger, down the back of the hand and wrist, and all the way to the elbow joint. This is an important line to maintain in the lower three positions.

Typical errors in the wrist position are the famous "pancake" wrist and the overly extended wrist.

The "pancake wrist."

The overly-extended wrist.

Note:

There is some disagreement as to whether the heel of the hand should touch the shoulder of the violin in the third position. As a matter of theory, probably not, however, in practice most of us do so, at least some of the time. The size of one's hand plays some role in this, as a larger hand will have a greater tendency to touch the shoulder. As a matter of opinion, this should not represent a significant issue.

PLACING THE FINGERS ON THE STRING

To understand how the fingers meet the string, try a well-known Dounis exercise with a pencil.

1. *Hold a pencil with your right hand, and place it between the left thumb and index finger.*

2. *Place the first finger on the pencil.*

3.   *One by one, as if playing B, C#, D, and E on the A string, add the other fingers.*

The finger action is initiated at the base joint of the finger. As each finger is placed on the pencil, feel the hand rotate to the left. Notice that as the second and third fingers meet the pencil, they fall in parallel lines with one another. These parallel lines should form a 45° angle to the line of the pencil. Once the first three fingers are in position, let the fourth finger fall naturally where it will. There will be some variation from player to player in the way the fourth finger falls to meet the pencil. This variation has much to do with the length and shape of the "pinky."

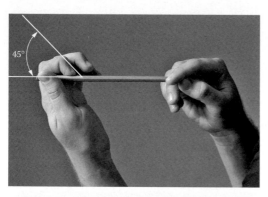 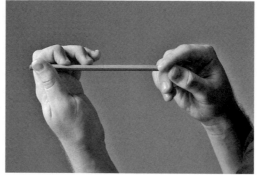

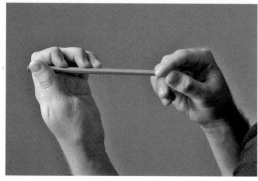 

Now substitute the violin for the pencil.

1. *Establish the hand position. First, align the neck of the instrument with the marks on the thumb and index finger (imaginary or real) as described above.*
2. *Form the V-shaped thumb position.*
3. *Bring each finger to the A string, as in the pencil exercise. Make sure the line from the first joint of the index finger to the elbow is clearly defined.*

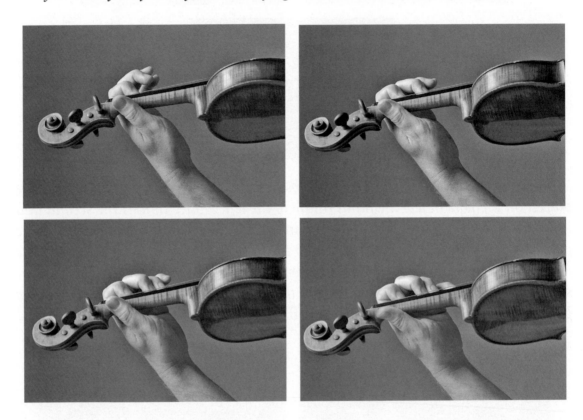

Observe the curvature of the fingers over the string and the parallel lines (at a 45° angle to the string line) formed by the fingers as they touch the string. Also notice the leftward rotation of the hand as each finger meets the string.

Remember that the finger action should be initiated by the base joints.

A simple way to establish the left hand setup is to play an octave in the first position (first finger E on the D string and fourth finger E on the A, for example). Keep the second and third fingers on the string behind the fourth finger. Make sure that the fourth finger is slightly arched. The hand will automatically assume its correct position. Notice that the thumb, wrist, and fingers conform without effort to the positions discussed above. As a matter of fact, one will find it extremely difficult to distort the hand position while holding the octave. The trick is to maintain this hand position all the time.

Here are three views of the hand frame formed by the first and fourth finger octave:

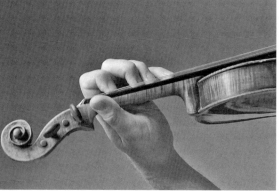

A common tendency is to round the back of the left hand. This distorts the position and, once again, affects the angle of the fingers on the string. Students who do this will play with their fingers too vertical to the string. Playing with a high thumb position is often the cause.

Avoid the rounded hand position

The hand position corrected

Remember, the back of the hand should appear flat, so that a line is formed from the first joint of the index finger to the elbow.

THE LEFT HAND AND ARM WHEN CHANGING STRINGS

Another important aspect of the left hand and arm involves moving from string to string. Notice that the wrist is held in a neutral position and a relatively straight line is formed from the hand to the elbow. This is the optimal position for the wrist in the first to third positions.

The proper alignment of the left arm and wrist

When we change strings, it is important to maintain the position of the wrist. This is done by using the *entire* arm, led by the movement of the elbow, to move from string to string.

These photographs show the arm position on the G string, the D string, the A string, and the E string.

Many students will break the wrist to change strings instead of using the entire arm. This is known as *ulnar deviation* and should be corrected. Remember, the wrist maintains its alignment with the forearm at all times.

An example of ulnar deviation

Notice how with ulnar deviation the position of the elbow is more appropriate for the D string rather than the E string.

Ulnar deviation is an easy error to miss, as we rarely watch violinists play from a vantage point from which it is visible. Breaking the wrist to change strings unnaturally twists the muscles in the arm, which can lead to tension or tendonitis. Furthermore, it distorts the hand position as well as the angle in which the fingers approach the string. The feeling of the finger patterns from string to string will also be inconsistent, negatively affecting the intonation.

Maintaining the proper position of the wrist helps to define the shape of the hand frame on every string. Doing so improves one's playing in almost every way.

THE ELBOW MOTION WHEN SHIFTING INTO THE HIGHER POSITIONS

As mentioned earlier, there are always three points of contact between the left hand and the violin. In the fourth position and above, those three points are the tip of the finger, the thumb, and the heel of the hand. As one shifts into the higher positions, the left hand moves up and over the top of the violin. The elbow initiates this movement by moving under the violin or to the right.

This motion is similar to the way the elbow moves to change strings in the lower positions, but now the movement is much more dramatic. In fact, the position of the elbow defines the feeling of position. Think of position not so much as a place on the fingerboard but rather as the physical placement of the elbow.

In these photographs, note the change of elbow position, first with the fingers on the G string, and then with the fingers on the E string.

When shifting to higher positions, the tendency is not to lead with the elbow to the position. When the elbow is not quite in place for the position, the result is that the first three fingers of the position are played, but then the elbow must move to accommodate the placement of the fourth finger. Eliminating this extra motion is important.

Of course, when one shifts back to a lower position, the elbow again leads the way, moving to the left as though pulling the hand back. Too often, a student will shift to a lower position without allowing the elbow to initiate the motion. The elbow remains in the upper position, while the left hand shifts down. Needless to say, the physical posture becomes very distorted. Usually, a severe case of ulnar deviation is the result.

These photographs show a shift downward in which the elbow is left in the upper position though the hand shifts down. Note the extreme ulnar deviation and the resulting distortion of the hand position.

Here is the corrected elbow position.

THE THUMB WHEN SHIFTING

The thumb position is the other important component of the left hand in the upper positions. As one moves to the higher positions, the thumb slides under the neck to the saddle of the instrument. The most critical point here is that the thumb *never* leaves the saddle, regardless of how high one plays on the fingerboard.

When moving to high positions the thumb must maintain contact with the saddle of the instrument.

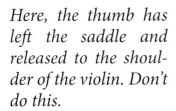

Here, the thumb has left the saddle and released to the shoulder of the violin. Don't do this.

The fact is, the thumb and index finger can *really* stretch apart, much more so than many imagine. This stretch is necessary in order to play at the top of the fingerboard and should be developed.

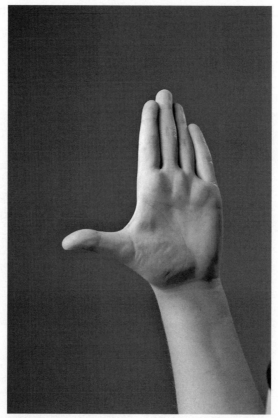

Stretch!

Releasing the thumb from the saddle to the shoulder should be avoided. Once the thumb leaves the saddle it no longer supports the finger pressure, and then, when shifting back to a lower position, one must lift the thumb back over the saddle, which is very awkward and most inefficient. Finally, leaving the saddle distorts the hand position, so that the angle of the fingers is too vertical in relation to the string.

Note:

In cases when one must play in extremely high positions, it is acceptable for players with small hands to release the thumb from the saddle to the side of the fingerboard, but not to the shoulder of the instrument. In keeping contact with the side of the fingerboard, the thumb can still slide easily into a lower position without having to lift over the saddle. That said, it is preferable to maintain contact with the saddle whenever possible.

THE ANGLE OF THE FINGERS THROUGH THE POSITIONS

The angle of the fingers is an important factor in the higher positions. We have discussed how the fingers are placed at a 45° angle to the line of the string. This angle does not change significantly, regardless of the position. It is true, the fingers generally become flatter the higher one plays, but the *angle* of the fingers to the line of the string stays the same.

The angle of the fingers to the line of the string is maintained in all positions

THE WEAK "PINKY"

The little finger, or "pinky," of the left hand is a notorious problem for young violinists (and not so young). There is no denying that the little finger is, by far, the weakest of the bunch. A weak pinky usually means collapsed finger joints, which the player compensates for by holding the little finger straight and rigid.

A weak pinky. Notice how the first joint has collapsed

As mentioned earlier, the little finger should have some arch while on the string. However, the degree of the arch can be slight, as long as it is there. One factor that affects the arch is where the string touches the finger. Be careful not to play too much on the fingertip. Using more of the pad on the fourth finger will result in a better tone.

Here is the correct position of the pinky. Notice that its shape is slightly arched

A good left hand will have a structured quality. With top players, the left hand has a muscular look, the shape of the hand is sharply defined, and the movements of the hand and arm are precise and efficient. Although it is possible to play with various distortions in the position (and many players do), making the effort to structure the position carefully will greatly facilitate technical mastery.

Now let's turn our attention to the bow grip.

4

Holding the Bow

It is often said that the art of violin playing lies in mastering the bow. Indeed, how we use the bow determines the character of our sound, the range of our expression, and the sparkle of our overall technique. To even a casual observer, a good bow arm appears (and is) completely natural, characterized by graceful, flowing movements. Yet this apparent ease is a matter of mastering many subtle movements in which muscles are trained to work in minute ways. Thus far, our discussion has addressed issues related to the left side of the body. Those issues will seem relatively simple and straightforward when compared to the complexities of bow technique.

Bow technique depends entirely upon how we hold the bow. Ideas about the best bow grip have changed considerably over the course of the past century. Carl Flesch, in his classic text from 1924, *The Art of Violin Playing,* identifies three schools of thought regarding the bow grip: the now antiquated German grip, the Russian grip, and the Franco-Belgian grip. Flesch, who initially advocated the Franco-Belgian grip, was immensely impressed at the time of writing his book by the level of violin playing coming from Russia, as exemplified by Jascha Heifetz, Mischa Elman, and Nathan Milstein. He expresses some uncertainty as to which bow grip might be most advantageous and muses that the Russian grip could result in a bigger sound with less effort.

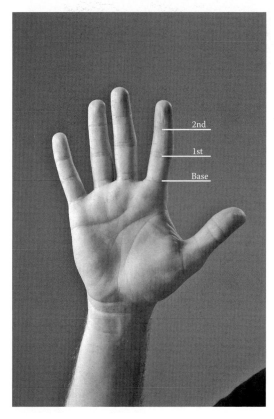

2nd
1st
Base

Photo by Patrick Neher

Interestingly, it is the Franco-Belgian grip that is dominant today and taught by most teachers worldwide. The advantage of this bow grip is its emphasis on the flexibility of *all* the finger joints. This flexibility is the key to a smooth, cohesive sound and seamless bow changes.

THE FRANCO-BELGIAN BOW GRIP

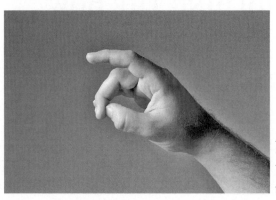

In the Franco-Belgian grip, the bow is held primarily with the thumb and the middle finger, while the other fingers serve to balance the grip. The middle finger and the thumb create a "teardrop" shape when holding the bow. The thumb is slightly bent and contacts the pad of the middle finger. The joints of the middle finger are curled but relaxed.

ESTABLISHING THE BASIC BOW GRIP WITH A PENCIL

1. *Hold your right hand out, palm up, fingers slightly apart. Place the pencil across the second joint of the index, middle, and ring fingers. The tip of the little finger should just touch the pencil.*

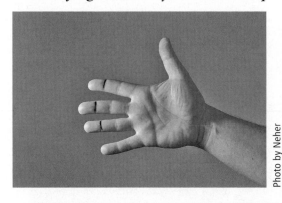
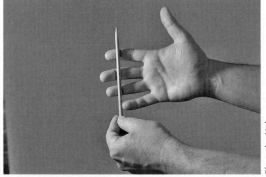

2. *Form the teardrop shape while holding the pencil between the tip of the thumb and the pad of the middle finger.*

3. *Curl the fingers around the pencil and bend the thumb slightly.*

Photo by Neher

4. *The teardrop shape should be clear in the hand.*

Photo by Neher

FINGER SPACING ON THE BOW

Before trying the grip with the bow, let's try another exercise that will demonstrate the spacing of the fingers in the grip.

Hold your right arm in front of you so that the forearm is parallel to the floor. Allow the hand to relax and drop from the wrist. The fingers should assume their natural spacing. When we hold the bow, we will try to maintain this spacing. Everyone will have slightly different spacing between the fingers.

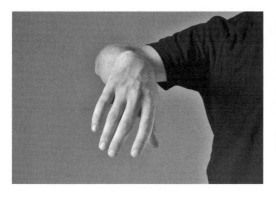 

Note:

It is important that the fingers be neither too close together nor too far apart. Deviating either way from the natural spacing of the fingers will cause the flexibility of the grip to be compromised.

Now try the grip with the bow:

1. *Place the bow across the first line of finger joints as in the pencil exercise.*

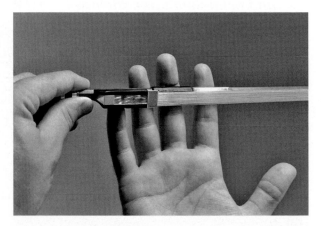

2. *Curl the fingers around the bow and place the thumb on the side of the stick just in front of where the frog begins. Keep the thumb slightly bent. The middle finger and thumb should be opposite one another, forming the basic teardrop shape discussed above.*

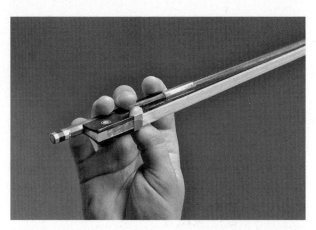

3. *Finally, turn the grip over so that the back of the hand is now facing up. Keep the fingers curled on the bow, especially the little finger. When the little finger is curled, the other fingers will follow suit without effort. Check the spacing of the fingers to see that they correspond with what you saw earlier, in the spacing exercise. The top of the hand should appear almost flat from the first joints of the fingers to the wrist.*

INDEX FINGER PLACEMENT

Where the index finger contacts the bow is critical to the Franco-Belgian grip. Many students err on this point. If we have carefully followed the steps outlined above, the bow should contact the index finger somewhere between the first and second joints. As a matter of practice, try to contact the stick closer to the second joint of the index finger. *The bow should never cross the line marking the first joint.*

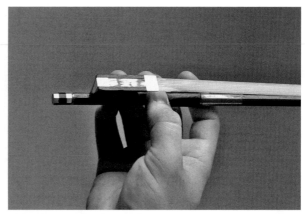
The proper index finger placement.

Many students place the bow between the base and first joint of the index finger. They do so because they feel they can produce more sound with the index finger "wrapped" around the bow. However, this greatly reduces the flexibility of the fingers. A student usually resorts to this index finger placement as a way of compensating for a poorly developed bow grip.

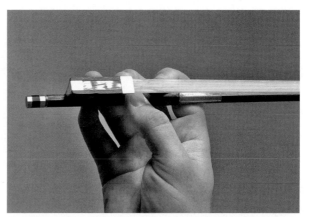
Here the stick crosses the first finger joint. Avoid this!

PRONATION

1. *Take hold of the middle of the bow with the left hand, making sure to keep the stick parallel to the floor.*

2. *Now, tilt the bow grip toward the tip of the bow. The fingers should form a 45° angle to the line of the stick.*

This tilting of the hand position is referred to as pronation. By pronating the fingers on the bow, we are able to transfer the weight of the right arm into the bow, and ultimately to the string, while still staying relaxed. It is possible to over-pronate. As a general rule of thumb, the angle of the fingers to the line of the stick should not exceed 45°.

THUMB COUNTERPRESSURE

When pronating the hand, the weight of the right arm is delivered primarily into the index finger while at the same

time the thumb provides counterpressure. The greater the force on the index finger, the more the thumb will push up to offer resistance.

To experience this sensation, hold the middle of the bow with the left hand, and grip the frog of the bow with only the right index finger and thumb. Push into the bow with the index finger and notice how the thumb automatically provides counterpressure. Notice that the thumb bends more or less, in response to the amount of force applied by the index finger.

This bending and straightening of the thumb is very important, and, finally, it corresponds to the volume of the sound — the thumb bends more when playing strongly and less when playing lightly. *The thumb is not fixed in one position.* Also, the

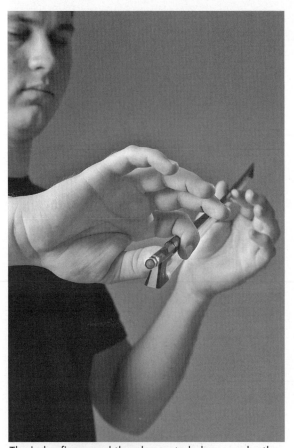

The index finger and thumb counterbalance each other.

degree of counterpressure is never excessive, but it is just enough to allow the weight of the arm to go into the string. A sign of too much counterpressure is if the tip of the thumb develops a flat (often, purple) indenture.

"CLINGING" FINGERS

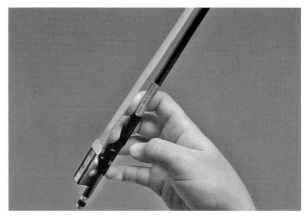

With the Franco-Belgian grip, the pads of the first, second, and third fingers "cling" to the bow. To really experience this sensation, see if you can hold the bow without using the thumb, making sure not to distort the grip or drop the bow while trying.

"Clinging" fingers are neither tense nor flaccid. Rather, the feeling is one of firmness. A firm but flexible grip is the key to a deep, sustained sound.

"Clinging fingers". Holding the bow without the thumb.

FINGER FLEXIBILITY

Finger flexibility is one of the most difficult techniques to master. The advantage of the Franco-Belgian grip is that all the joints of the hand are active. Finger flexibility is important for a smooth, cohesive sound; for soundless bow changes; and for many specific bow strokes, including spiccato and sautillé.

At a basic level, there are two fundamental finger positions that require sufficient flexibility: Curved fingers and extended fingers. The following exercise is a good way to learn these two finger positions:

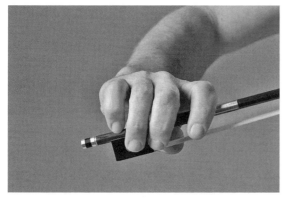

Curved fingers.

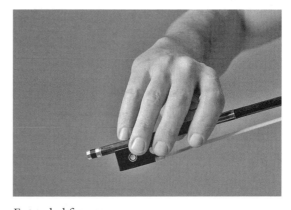

Extended fingers.

1. *Place the hand on a table with the joints curled under the hand. Make sure the tip of the thumb is touching the tip of the middle finger. The top of the hand should appear flat to the second line of finger joints.*

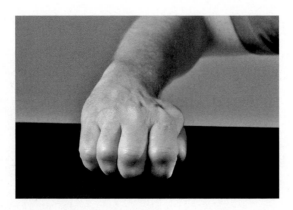

2. *Now, straighten the fingers, as if to lift the entire hand and arm off the table. Again, make sure the thumb continues to touch the middle finger.*

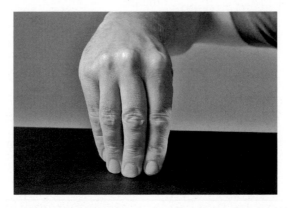

Try the same exercise without the table. This time, rotate the forearm toward your face (pronate). This is very close to the way the fingers work on the bow.

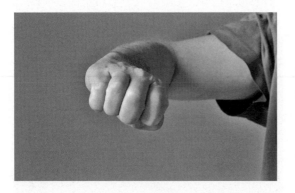 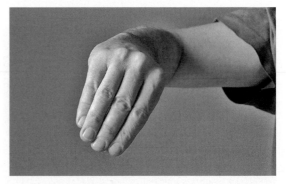

Still another good exercise is to try the curved finger/extended finger positions with a pencil in hand. If you do this correctly, you will quickly become aware of how much the little finger must work.

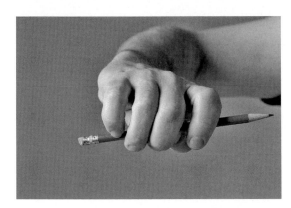 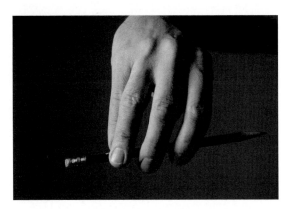

As we shall see in the next chapter, the curved finger/extended finger positions correspond to down bows and up bows.

THE LITTLE FINGER

Every violin teacher knows how difficult it is to train the little finger so that it easily assumes curved and extended positions. Years of teaching experience have taught me that the key to finger flexibility lies in developing the little finger. When the little finger curls and straightens, the other fingers follow.

The following "teeter-totter" exercise can help to strengthen the little finger:

1. *To begin, hold the bow in the middle of the stick. Extend the arm. Keep both the arm and the bow parallel to the floor. Make sure the little finger is curled.*

2. *Now, see if you can move the frog of the bow toward the floor by straightening the little finger.*

   This exercise is easier to do while holding the bow in the middle of the stick. Try it at the frog.

Note:

The little finger should rest on the "inside" facet of the bow, the nail actually resting on top of the stick. This will help keep the little finger from falling off the stick when it curls and straightens.

FEELING BALANCE AND WEIGHT

As we draw the bow across the string, the feeling of weight and the balance of the grip change. The following exercise will help you become aware of this.

1. *Hold the bow out in front of you, arm and bow both parallel to the floor. The weight of the bow should be felt in the little finger (make sure the little finger is curled).*

2. *Flip the bow over. Now the weight is felt in the index finger.*

Try the same exercise, but this time begin with the index finger off the bow. When you flip the bow over, take the little finger off.

This demonstration approximates the feeling of the bow, first at the frog and then at the tip. When playing at or near the frog, the weight of the bow is felt mainly in the little finger. Toward the tip, we feel the weight in the index finger. As we bow from frog to tip, the feeling of the weight gradually moves from the little finger to the index finger.

Draw a bow, beginning at the frog but without the index finger on the stick. As you move toward the tip, gradually place the index finger on the bow and lift the little finger off. Reverse the process to go up bow. Feel how the weight of the bow is transferred from the little finger to the index finger and back again.

ROLLING THE BOW BETWEEN THE THUMB AND MIDDLE FINGER

By rolling the bow between the thumb and the middle finger while playing, we can manipulate the amount of bow hair on the string — to keep the hair either flat to the string or turned to the side, depending on the musical circumstance.

As a simple exercise, see if you can roll the bow back and forth between the thumb and the middle finger while maintaining the integrity of the grip. Then, try to do so while playing down and up bow.

Note:

Learn to use the thumb and the middle finger to adjust how much hair is on the string. Try to avoid breaking the wrist to accomplish this. We will discuss this further in Chapter 6.

CONCLUSION

Achieving a successful bow grip requires considerable care and patience. The finger movements of a good bow grip are very sophisticated and require extensive training of the muscles of the hand. When learning how to hold the bow, one must constantly strive to maintain good form while at the same time developing the necessary finger flexibility characteristic of the Franco-Belgian bow grip.

In the following chapters, we will further examine issues relating to the bow grip and, more generally, to developing a good bow arm.

5

PUTTING RIGHT AND LEFT TOGETHER

One of the singular difficulties for string players is that right and left are doing radically different tasks. Playing the violin is a bit like rubbing your tummy while patting your head and jumping on one foot all at the same time.

Up until this point, we have examined right and left separately. Now, let's put the two together.

"HOME" POSITION OR THE "MAGIC SQUARE"

As we bring the bow to the string, our first consideration is to find the "home" position, which is determined when the bow is placed on the string *approximately* in the middle of the bow.

Why is "home" the middle of the bow? One reason is that many bow strokes are played in the middle or begin from the middle. More importantly, though, everything that happens in violin playing is a departure from this elemental position. The middle of the bow is a point of orientation from which the bow arm either extends (in moving toward the tip) or folds (as one bows toward the frog). When we place the bow in the home position, the weight of the arm should be transferred effortlessly into the bow.

The home position is not necessarily the true middle of the bow, but rather, *the point at which the forearm forms a right angle to the upper arm.* When this right angle is established, the upper arm will form a parallel line with the bow, and the forearm a parallel line with both the fingerboard of the violin and the floor. A near perfect square should be clear. This is often

The home position

referred to as the "magic square" because of its fundamental importance to good bow technique. The terms *home position* and *magic square* essentially refer to the same idea, but it is helpful to think of the home position forming the shape of the magic square.

Obviously, players with longer arms will place the bow above the true middle of the bow, and those with shorter arms below. Remember, the home position is not an actual point on the bow, but rather a physical posture.

THE STRING PLANE

The "string plane" is a term that describes the level of the bow arm while playing on a given string. It is helpful to understand this concept as an imaginary plane extending into space. The string plane is most clearly defined when the upper arm is on the same level as the bow. This will be determined by the position of the elbow.

The string plane

We can further illustrate this idea with the following exercise:

1. *Place the bow on the G string in the home position. Make sure that the parallel lines of the magic square are clear and, in particular, that the forearm is parallel to the floor.*

2. *Move to the D string, but do so by lowering the entire right arm as a unit so that the shape of the magic square is maintained. To do this, one must use the upper arm to lift the arm to the G string.*

3. *Now, move to the A string, this time feeling the whole arm drop while maintaining the form of the magic square.*

4. *And finally, move to the E string.*

Note:

The position of the elbow is the key to defining the string plane. As we draw the bow down and up on a particular string, the height of the elbow should not change. This is very important.

The idea of the string plane is very clear if we do this exercise at the tip of the bow. In this case, the arm must move as a unit in order to change strings.

Now, try the exercise at the frog of the bow. Be sure to change strings with the entire arm.

There is no hard rule as to exactly how high the elbow (and consequently the upper arm) should be in relation to the bow. Some violinists play with the elbow on a perfect plane with the bow. Others will elevate the elbow to some degree, and still others will play with the elbow slightly below the level of the bow.

High elbow   Neutral elbow   Lower elbow

Another view:

High elbow   Neutral elbow   Lower elbow

These subtle differences are something players should explore, as each can change the quality of the sound produced and also affect the basic sensation of moving the bow. The important point is that *each string represents a different string plane.* As one draws the bow from frog to tip on that string, the height of the elbow, whatever that is, should remain consistent. The elbow position determines the string plane.

It is a very common mistake to allow the elbow height to fall as one plays toward the tip, so that the level of the arm falls below the level of the bow. When this occurs, its effect is that the weight of the arm is no longer transferred to the string, and, consequently, the quality of the sound is immediately diminished.

The ability to maintain the elbow height as one goes toward the tip is really a matter of training the deltoid muscle to hold the arm up throughout the bow stroke. This is not easy at first, and a player learning to do so may actually experience some soreness in the upper arm for a short time until the deltoid muscle strengthens.

As the bow travels to the tip, the level of arm…   …falls below the level of the bow at tip   Here, the elbow is corrected

The opposite problem, equally undesirable, is for the elbow height to fall as one nears the frog. This is a most common error, and, unfortunately, something many students are taught to do.

The level of arm in middle of bow…   …falling as near the frog…   The elbow position is corrected

This mistake, which is easy to correct, will be explored more fully in the next section. In brief, the elbow falls because the player leads to the frog with the wrist. Breaking the wrist to get to the frog automatically lowers the elbow.

Again, this effectively takes the weight of the arm out of the bow. When we move the bow to the frog with the *upper arm* while not breaking the wrist, the elbow height is maintained and the weight of the arm stays on the string.

DRAWING A FULL BOW IN THREE STEPS

Keeping in mind the importance of a clearly defined string plane, we may now turn our attention to drawing the bow. There are just three major muscular movements that go into drawing the down bow:

1. *Beginning from the frog, the first movement is initiated from the shoulder. The right elbow moves* laterally *about four or five inches, though the bow moves about one-quarter of the way down.*

2. *Next, the forearm unfolds from the elbow joint. This movement carries the bow roughly three-quarters of the way toward the tip.*

3. *In the last movement, the arm straightens. The movement again is felt in the shoulder or upper arm. In order to keep the bow straight, it is important to push the arm forward, or out, to the front of the body. This can be difficult for a student to do at first.*

Here is another view of these basic movements.

When going up bow, the three steps are reversed, as follows:

1. *The upper arm pulls back, or in, and the elbow joint bends slightly.*
2. *The forearm folds from the elbow joint as the bow travels to the lower quarter. Be sure not to let the elbow fall.*
3. *Finally, the upper arm pushes the bow up and back to the frog. This movement comes from the shoulder.*

Note:

This last step is frequently lacking in young players and is the reason why they are unable to get all the way to the frog. The ability to use the lower quarter of the bow has a tremendous effect on the volume of the sound.

TRIANGLE–SQUARE–TRIANGLE

When we draw the bow from frog to tip well, three basic geometric shapes will be clearly defined: triangle, square, and triangle. Awareness of these shapes is yet another way to realize physically the subtle movements that go into developing a good bow arm.

1.   *When at the frog, a triangle is formed by the upper arm, the forearm, and an imaginary line from where the bow contacts the string to the shoulder joint.*

2.   *The square is defined at the midpoint of the bow (remember, this is the home position).*

3.   *Finally, another triangle is established when we reach the end of the bow. It is formed by the line of the bow itself, a line from right index finger to the shoulder joint, and a line from the shoulder joint to the point where the bow contacts the string.*

FINDING THE "TRUE TIP" OF THE BOW

It is helpful to determine exactly where the tip exists for each player. This will not necessarily be at the end of the bow for everyone. Violinists with long arms will have no difficulty getting to the tip of the bow. For smaller players and children, however, it can be impossible to play to the tip without pulling the bow around and behind.

To find the "true tip" of the bow, play a down bow following the three steps outlined earlier. When the final step is completed, check to see if the bow is still parallel to the bridge. The "true tip" is the point where the player can go no further without pulling the bow around and behind, or "crooked." (We will discuss "crookedness" later in the chapter.)

Here, the player pulls bow around and behind to reach the tip

The true tip for the player

This player has no difficulty reaching the actual tip of the bow

THE LATERAL PLACEMENT OF THE VIOLIN

Where the violin is placed on the collarbone (see Chapter 2) will affect how far one can go toward the tip of the bow. If the violin is held more in front of

The player is holding the violin too far toward the shoulder, making it difficult draw a straight bow

By moving the violin more toward the front of the bow direction, which should be parallel to the bridge, is corrected

the body, it will be easier to go further toward the tip. As we move the violin toward the shoulder, it becomes increasingly difficult to reach the tip because the bow arm must move to the front of the body, which requires greater extension to get to the tip.

Taller violinists usually feel more comfortable holding the violin a little more toward the shoulder. This opens the posture and allows for more freedom of motion with the bow arm. Smaller players will benefit by moving the violin in, toward the center of the posture.

There is no hard rule regarding the lateral placement of the violin. However, moving the violin to a different position, either more toward the shoulder or more toward the front of the body, will probably require some adaptation or change of the chinrest and shoulder pad. Be open to the possibilities, and experiment until the bow arm and violin placement are working together optimally.

THE ALIGNMENT OF THE BOW TO THE VIOLIN

Bow alignment is the single most important factor in the kind of sound we produce. It also dramatically affects the free, fluid movements required in the various bow strokes. Working to develop a precise line of travel for the bow is not unlike the pursuit for the perfect golf swing or tennis stroke. Mastering bow alignment can seem complicated, but the goal is quite simple: *Bow straight.* Bowing straight, at a fundamental level, means keeping the bow parallel to the bridge throughout the bow stroke. This is easier said than done.

"CROOKED" BOWING

"Crooked" bowing is a ubiquitous problem for violinists. Nearly all of us must confront this tendency at some point in our development. Unfortunately, crooked bowing is quite natural. When we bow crooked, the arm inscribes an arc that travels around and behind the player. The arm likes to do this. It feels comfortable, and, after all, the arm "lives" on the side of the body — it just wants to return there!

"Crooked" bowing beginning at frog ...   ... and going to the tip.

The corrected arc from frog to ...   ... The tip.

In fact, to bow straight, the arm draws an arc outward toward the *front* of the body, in exactly the opposite direction. Initially, this feels strange, but once mastered it helps to keep the bow parallel to the bridge.

CONTACT POINT

Straight bowing, more than anything else, relates to one's ability to hold a given contact point, without the slightest deviation, throughout both the down and up bow. Contact point is a very simple concept — it is the point between the bridge and the fingerboard where the bow contacts the string.

A controlled contact point is the single most important element in a player's sound production, and the ability to maintain that point throughout the bow results in an even, sustained sound. Any deviation from the contact point will have a negative effect on the sound.

Measuring from the bridge to the fingerboard, we can define five possible contact points, each one being the width of the bow hair. These photographs show the five possible contact points.

A skilled violinist utilizes all the contact points to create a palette of tonal color. The sound gets louder as we go closer to the bridge and softer as we move toward the fingerboard. A strong projected concerto sound will necessarily be quite close to the bridge, whereas a *sotto voce* passage will be played closer to the fingerboard. Even within a given phrase, a player might change the contact point several times. When an even, sustained sound is required, it is critical to hold the contact point without any deviation.

In many respects, learning to hold the contact point poses one of the most challenging technical problems for students. It is a skill that is not emphasized enough by many teachers. Holding the contact point is *very* difficult and entails ultra-precise movements of the bow arm musculature.

Once the basic movements that constitute drawing the bow are comfortable, a player can apply those movements to maintaining the contact point. Eventually, after much trial and error, the direction of the bow arm is refined

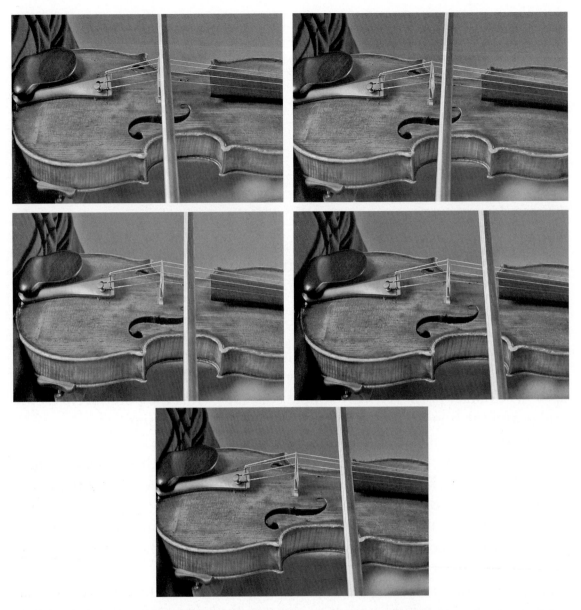

and the contact point mastered. There is a particular feeling to playing with a flawless contact point. Some describe it as a sense of "cutting" into the string, and others feel it as a kind of "friction" generated by the bow hair. However conceptualized, controlling the contact point is the key to a great sound.

Note:

A controlled contact point = a beautiful, sustained tone!

POSTURE REVISITED

Up to this point, this chapter has addressed how the bow meets the violin. Now that we have put left and right together, another look at posture is in

Good standing posture in the 'home' position

Good sitting posture in the 'home' position

Another example…

order. In Chapter 1, we discussed general principles that constitute good posture and bad habits that one should avoid. Once we assume the playing position, it is very easy to fall into poor postural habits. In fact, constant vigilance is required to maintain good postural habits throughout a violinist's playing career.

We can check the posture from the home position. Remember the fundamentals of good alignment: ears over shoulders, shoulders over hips, hips over the knees and feet. Chest is open and lifting. Shoulders are relaxed. The chin is lowered to meet the chinrest, but the head maintains its alignment with the center of the body. Try not to turn the head too far to the left.

The arms are suspended up and away from the body, but the shoulders do not lift. The violin is held parallel to the floor. The right forearm is parallel to the floor. The "magic square" is clearly defined.

Whew! If you can do all that and still play, you're doing well!

SOME COMMON POSTURAL FAULTS

1. *The head turns excessively to the left, creating tension in the neck (neck muscle will bulge out).*

2. *The head angles away from the violin.*

3. *The head angles toward the violin.*

4. *The arms fall toward the side of the body, the violin angles toward the floor, and the bow arm droops from the magic square as the elbow falls.*

5. *The shoulders are raised and rounded forward.*

6. *The knees are hyperextended and the posture is swaybacked.*

7. While sitting, the posture slumps.

8. While sitting, the posture twists.

Good postural habits create a playing position that is free and allows for a maximum efficiency of movement. Poor postural habits lead to chronic tension that can, over time, begin to feel normal. Poor posture can also cause muscles to work against one another. In this case, the instrument *feels difficult* to play. When one watches a great violinist play, the ease of playing is readily apparent: the posture is relaxed and the playing motion looks fluid and effortless — because it is.

TENSION AND RELEASE

In reality, it is impossible to play the violin while being relaxed all the time. Muscular effort creates tension. The trick is to be aware of when and how the tension occurs and to release it as soon as possible. For example, a long shift up the G string produces some tension as the shoulder and head support the instrument in order to free the hand for the shift. However, as soon as the shift is completed, the head and shoulder must release. One can facilitate the release by taking the head off the chinrest from time to time and letting the violin rest in the left hand. (I like to show my students videos of David Oistrakh, as he frequently lifts his head away from the instrument while playing.)

There are other types of tension, some quite subtle, that may hinder a player. For example, many violinists place the fingers on the string with too much force. The remedy is to release the pressure of the finger immediately after it contacts the string. Find the minimum amount of pressure required to play the note. Squeezing the neck of the instrument with the thumb is another problem, as we have already discussed. Another common malady is for the right index finger and thumb to press with too much force into the bow. Experiment by seeing how much sound you can generate from the string while keeping the thumb and index finger completely relaxed. Difficult passages or very aggressive music also can create tension. Learning *right effort,* or the appropriate physical effort, is the key in this case.

> **Note:**
>
> Too often, we associate difficulty with muscular effort. Right effort is a matter of reducing one's physical effort to the minimum required to play a passage well — no more, no less.

Unreleased tension not only limits one's ability but can also lead to chronic problems such as tendonitis and carpal tunnel syndrome. Although simply overusing the muscles can cause these debilitating physical problems, unreleased tension will greatly contribute to them. As a general observation, violin playing requires the subtle rather than the gross use of muscles. Male violin students, in particular, are often guilty of using far too much muscle to play, which of course causes tension.

Tension is unavoidable, but the principles of release and right effort will help you cope.

6

More on Bowing

In Chapter 3 we examined the bow grip in detail and in Chapter 5 we discussed the integration of the bow arm and the violin position. Let's now take a closer look at the finer points of bow technique.

Have some one keep the bow from moving in this exercise

PUSH AND PULL

There are two basic sensations when drawing the bow: pushing and pulling. In the section in Chapter 3 on finger flexibility, we discussed the two essential finger positions, curved and extended. This idea can now be applied to down bows and up bows.

When we begin the down bow, the sensation is of *pulling* the bow. Conversely, with the up bow we *push* the bow. *To illustrate this point vividly, place the bow on the D string (in the midpoint of the bow) while someone else holds the bow in place.*

The pulling action on the up bow. The fingers are curled

The pushing action on the up bow. Here, the fingers extend

Try to draw a down bow, allowing the fingers to flex into the curled position. Feel the pulling sensation, which will be quite exaggerated. Now change direction and go up bow. Here, the sensation is felt as pushing, and the fingers flex into the extended position.

One can continue the exercise further if the assisting person continues to hold the bow but allows it to move somewhat. Enough resistance to the moving bow should be applied to accentuate the sensation of push and pull. Gradually, the resistance can be lessened while the player continues to push and pull.

> **Note:**
>
> While doing this exercise, it is important that the fingers of the bow grip pronate at a 45° angle to the line of the stick, as described in Chapter 3. This angle does not change as the fingers flex between the curled and extended positions.

Notice that the fingers curl or extend more as greater resistance is applied and less when there is little resistance. This corresponds to playing either strongly or softly. In other words, the stronger the sound, the deeper the fingers will curl. When playing more softly, the fingers will tend to be more extended. However, the flexing between the extended and curled position continues, even if the movement is minute.

Finger position for an aggressive sound

Finger position for a softer sound

A simple way to describe the idea of push and pull is that the fingers curl on the down bow and extend on the up bow.

THE BOW CHANGE

The movement of the fingers from curled to extended position is the basis for the bow change. Regardless of where we are in the bow, the fingers of the bow react to the change of direction. When we change from an up bow to a down bow, the fingers will assume the curled position; they will extend when changing from down bow to up bow.

Finger position on the up bow approaching the tip...

...and finger position after changing down bow

Finger position on the down bow, approaching the tip...

...and the finger position after changing up bow

It is important that the finger movement not be loose or sloppy, resulting in the bow being thrown or flipped at the change. Instead, the movement of the fingers should be just enough to "catch" the change of direction. Think of the way shock absorbers work on a car as it goes over a bump. The change of bow is a sort of bump that the finger movement absorbs.

When learning the finger movements for the bow change, it is helpful to exaggerate the curled and extended positions in order to develop the muscles. In time, the movement can be gradually decreased until it is apparent mainly in the little finger.

Exactly at what point the fingers curl or extend when changing bows is a subject of some controversy. Some teachers

As this player approaches the frog...

...he breaks the wrist to make the bow change. Avoid this!

teach that the fingers curl or extend to meet the change of direction, or just *before* the bow change. There is nothing wrong with this idea, but experiencing the movement of the fingers *as a result* of the bow's changing direction is a more organic approach, requiring virtually no effort once the muscles are trained. A common metaphor that describes the bow change is to liken the movement to the bristles on a paint-

Here, the wrist position is creect at the point of the bow change

brush as one paints back and forth. The bristles of the brush change direction *after* the painter initiates the movement in the new direction.

The most important point to remember about the bow change is that it is controlled *completely* by the fingers.

Many violinists learn to make the bow change from the wrist instead of with the fingers. Although changing bows with the wrist can work to some extent, it is not desirable to do so. The moment we break the wrist, the weight of the arm is no longer transferred to the bow. This, of course, affects the sound. The following exercise demonstrates the point:

1. *Place the bow in the lower half on the D string with the wrist in its proper position — that is, so the top of the hand faces your nose. Feel the weight of the arm as it is transferred to the bow.*

2. *Now, break the wrist so that the top of the hand faces toward the scroll of the violin. Notice how the feeling of weight being transferred into the bow is lost.*

Breaking the wrist to change bows is usually an attempt to compensate for lack of finger flexibility. A student can get by for quite a long time doing this, but eventually the lack of finger flexibility will reveal major problems, especially in regard to more difficult bow strokes such as spiccato. Furthermore, breaking the wrist causes one to play on the side of the hair, rather than the flat, which again lessens the volume of the sound.

Students who break the wrist as they approach the frog can benefit from the following exercise:

Draw a smiley face on the top of your right hand.
Play a down bow and an up bow. The smiley face should always appear to be looking at your nose. If you break the wrist, the smiling face will look in another direction.

Another common problem related to the bow change is the tendency to avoid the frog. Once again, this is usually a question of poorly developed finger flexibility. The frog is the heaviest part of the bow, and consequently the most difficult to control. If the bow change is not working well (that is, the fingers are not flexing to absorb the shock of the change), the sound suffers as one approaches the frog. The easy solution for a student is to avoid the frog altogether.

As we discussed in Chapter 3, the little finger is the key to the curled and extended positions. If the little finger bends for the down bow, the other fingers automatically follow. Using *all* of the bow, especially the quarter nearest the frog, greatly affects the amount of sound produced.

Finally, a good bow change is defined by the sound one hears. Does the tone remain consistent through the change, or does it get softer as one nears the frog? Is there a break in the sound? Is there an accent or a "click"? Is the change seamless? Let your ears guide your work.

USING THE WRIST TO CHANGE STRINGS

In Chapter 4, we explored the concept of the string plane and emphasized that moving from string to string requires the entire arm to move as a unit. The exception to this is when we move back and forth between two or three strings in quick succession.

From Partita III by J.S. Bach

In this musical passage, from Partita III by J. S. Bach, changing strings with the whole arm would be very difficult, perhaps nearly impossible (though I have seen it attempted). In this case, we use the wrist to make the quick changes from string to string.

To try the basic movement required in changing strings with the wrist, hold your right arm up, forearm parallel to the floor. Let the hand fall from the wrist, and then raise the hand, again from the wrist, above the level of the arm.

The exercise looks as though you are waving goodbye to someone as the hand moves up and down. Notice that when the hand falls, the fingers tend to extend, and when the hand is raised, the fingers curl. This action is important to the change of string and further underscores the importance of developing the flexibility of the fingers.

When we change from a lower string to a higher string, the hand falls from the wrist and the fingers extend. Going the other direction, higher to lower, the hand is raised and the fingers curl. In either case, the level of the bow arm (as defined by the height of the elbow) should not change. The wrist does all the work.

Now try the up-and-down movement of the hand while playing this musical example.

The 'up' position of the hand while playing on the D string

The 'down' position while on the A string

When the notes are slurred, the up-and-down motion of the hand is obvious. However, when the notes are separate, as in a passage played détaché, the action becomes more complicated.

In this case, the up-and-down movement is accompanied by the movement of the forearm. The composite creates a clear circular movement working clockwise.

The clockwise movement comes quite naturally to us. In most cases, violinists will bow rapid string crossings in this way. But, on occasion, we must play something requiring the movement to go the opposite direction, or counterclockwise.

The primary sensation in this example is of the hand lifting to the level of the D string. The counterclockwise movement is considerably more difficult than the clockwise.

THE ELEMENTS OF TONE PRODUCTION: CONTACT POINT, WEIGHT, AND BOW SPEED

Assuming that the mechanics of the bow arm are in good order, tone production depends on the interplay of three fundamental elements: the contact point (which we have already discussed in some detail), the degree of weight into the string, and the speed of the bow. These aspects of bow technique create the palette of tonal color for every violinist. As a matter of practice, a skilled player constantly varies the relationship of contact point, weight, and bow speed in subtle ways to reflect a given musical idea. Let's briefly examine how these three elements work in tandem with one another.

In Chapter 4, we identified five possible contact points between the bridge and the fingerboard. A given tone can be made louder by moving the contact point closer to the bridge.

As we play closer to the bridge, we will apply more weight and less speed to the string in order to keep the tone from losing its focus. In fact, if we play very close to the bridge, say on the first contact point, we can apply a great deal of weight into the string, but we also must move the bow very slowly to maintain the sound. Playing closer to the bridge produces an edge to the sound, similar to saying *eeeeeeeeeeeeeee*. It is a cutting tone that projects well and for this reason is often used when playing concertos with orchestra.

As we move the contact point midway between the bridge and the fingerboard, we can move the bow faster and use less weight since the string tension softens as we move away from the bridge. On this contact point the tone tends more toward an *oooooooooo* sound, or an open, resonant tone that is more singing than the *eeeeeeeee* tone.

Of course, if the contact point is moved all the way to the fingerboard, the sound becomes airy and superficial, lacking focus. One will play close to the fingerboard to create a particular effect suggested by the music.

When playing in very high positions, the string length shortens considerably, and its vibration is greatly reduced. This requires that one play very close to the bridge but with hardly any weight — exactly the opposite of what we do in the lower positions. Finding the exact relationship of weight, speed, and contact point is much more difficult in the high positions, especially when the passage is marked forte.

Most of the time, speed and weight are adjusted to accommodate the chosen contact point. However, we can increase the volume of the sound just by adding either speed or weight to a given contact point. Of the two, using speed to produce more volume is preferable to applying more weight — added speed increases the string's vibration and tends to open the sound, whereas more weight does the reverse and can actually reduce the sound. The optimal amount of weight going into the string should be just enough to keep the string freely vibrating.

Experimenting with contact point, weight, and speed opens up a world of tonal variation for a player. However, it is important to emphasize that a violinist must have complete control of the bow direction — meaning the ability to bow parallel to the bridge with no variation in the contact point — in order to explore this world successfully.

"CUTTING" THE STRING

The string is round, and it also vibrates in a circular pattern. Because of this, there are really two sides of the string on which we can play, the front side and the back side. It is good to think of playing on the side of the string rather than on the top, or its surface. This idea can lead to the sensation of "cutting" the string, or of generating friction against the vibration of the string, which actually further enhances the string's continuous vibration.

In certain circumstances, as in playing forte on the G string, we can take this idea even further by playing on one side of the string on the down bow and the other side on the up bow. Again, this encourages the feeling of "cutting" the sound from the string. The idea of "cutting" the string should not be confused with a harsh, scratchy sound. Rather, its effect is to produce a slight edge to the tone while maximizing the string's vibration.

WEIGHT VERSUS PRESSURE

Often, the terms weight and pressure are used interchangeably. The difference between the two is more conceptual than anything else. Perhaps the word *weight* conveys a healthier approach to sound production than the word *pressure*. Pressure implies pressing or crushing, which, of course, produces an ugly, scratchy sound and also is associated with added physical tension. The idea of weight conjures an image of something more relaxed, even passive. I prefer using the word *weight* for this reason, as the goal for every player should be to produce a beautiful tone with minimum effort.

ATTACK AND RELEASE

Every note begins with some sort of attack. The word *attack* implies something aggressive, but in this case, not always so. Attack refers to the front, or beginning, of a note. Attack defines a note's dynamic character and starts the string vibrating. An attack can range from a note that begins with a very strong accent to one that has none at all. In between exist countless variations. The attack should be followed by a release, which then frees the string to vibrate. If one begins a note with a strong accent but does not follow it with a release, the resulting tone is pressed and scratchy. The release produces a full, open sound.

A good way to practice the idea of the attack is to place the bow on the string (experiment with various parts of the bow) and wiggle the string back and forth while not actually making a sound. The degree of grip you feel through the bow is the basis for the attack — the greater the grip, the stronger the attack. Next, grip the string and play a note, making sure to release the force generated by the grip of the string. The sound produced should be a "click" or a "pop." You should also notice that the fingers flex slightly as they release the attack.

INCREASING THE DEGREE OF THE ATTACK

To increase the degree of the attack, one can apply more vertical force into the string or increase the speed of the bow. Although one does both to some extent depending on the musical circumstances, developing the ability to move the bow quickly at the beginning of a note greatly enhances the quality of the attack. The use of speed rather than vertical force tends to "launch" a note from the instrument. Vertical force actually can suppress the resonance of a note. In the case of a note with no accent, the attack of the note is generated by the use of speed alone — the bow moves slightly faster at the beginning of the note to start the string vibrating but then slows to sustain the note.

THE RELEASE

The concept of the release is developed best if isolated from the attack. The release can be thought of as the *base tone*. Depending on the musical passage, the base tone might be forte or piano, but in either case a freely vibrating string should characterize the tone. One can practice this simply by playing a note while trying to maximize the vibration of the string. The D string is a good string to work with since it is very easy to see the string vibrate. The goal is to generate a free, unforced tone.

Notice when doing this exercise that pressing into the string reduces its vibration. For solo playing, the base tone will not vary much in actual volume because a soloist must always project the sound. Dynamic intensity and contrast come from what one does with the beginning of the notes, or the attack.

DEVELOPING THE ATTACK

The idea of attack and release is that every note begins with a front, or an attack, which then is released to the base tone. An effective exercise that develops this technique is to play a given note up bow and down bow (it is not necessary to use the whole bow), beginning with an even, unaccented tone. Gradually, start adding slight accents to each change of bow, slowly increasing their intensity.

Make sure the bow speed at the beginning of each note corresponds to the degree of the accent. As the accents increase in intensity, more and more vertical force will come into play. Following each accent, release the sound to the base tone and allow the bow speed to slow somewhat as the tone is sustained. The longer the note is sustained, the more the bow speed will slow.

In an effort to develop tonal intensity, students often resort to pressing the sound throughout the bow stroke. Usually this is characterized by a slow, even bow speed and virtually no release. The result is an unpleasant, scratchy sound. Learning the technique of attack and release is the key to dynamic intensity and contrast. It also ensures that the tone quality stays beautiful.

7

VIBRATO

Vibrato is as unique to each individual as is handwriting. The fast, intense vibrato of Jascha Heifetz or the sweet, singing vibrato of Itzhak Perlman is immediately recognizable to a listener. Vibrato defines the personality of a violinist more than any other single factor. It is also perhaps the most important expressive tool available to a player.

Learning vibrato is similar to learning how to ride a bike. Just as riding a bike with training wheels cannot teach the feeling of balance necessary to ride, similarly, all the instruction and exercises in the world do little more than describe vibrato. Vibrato is one of those things we just "get" one day. Of course, teachers must "teach" vibrato, but it is good to recognize that in the end, students discover the *feeling* of vibrato for themselves.

A student first learning vibrato must train the muscles of the left arm to produce very minute movements. It is important to realize it takes time to strengthen these muscles enough so that the vibrato motion can begin. Although a student needs to understand the basic mechanics of a good vibrato, it is through trial and error that vibrato is *discovered*.

WRIST VERSUS ARM

There are two basic types of vibrato, wrist and arm. Either one can be successful. As students first learn vibrato, they naturally gravitate to one type or the other. As a matter of opinion, a teacher should allow for this and not insist on one particular type of vibrato. In fact, wrist and arm vibratos have more in common with one another than differences, as we will see in the following sections.

Understanding these similarities might lead a violinist to develop both an arm and wrist vibrato, or a combination of the two. Carl Flesch advocates this approach to vibrato in his book *The Art of Violin Playing*. He writes that a combination vibrato has the greatest expressive potential.

THE THUMB HINGE

The key to a good vibrato, whether it be wrist or arm, lies in developing the motion of the thumb hinge. The thumb hinge occurs at the base joint of the thumb. It allows the hand to move back and forth while the thumb itself is stationary. To discover the thumb hinge, try the following exercise:

Take hold of your left thumb with your right hand. Keep the left thumb straight and bent slightly outward (the V position described in Chapter 3).
Now, move the hand back and forth as if waving to someone while holding the thumb still with your right hand. The thumb hinge should be readily apparent.

The photographs show this exercise from two perspectives.

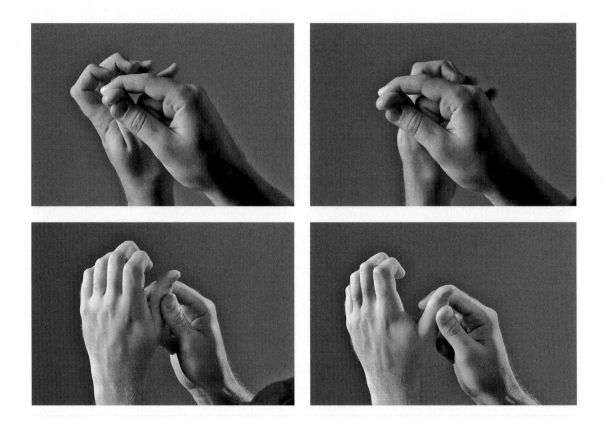

The flexibility of the thumb hinge is the basis for a good vibrato. Try the exercise first by initiating the waving movement of the hand from the wrist, and then from the elbow. Notice that, though the waving motion is initiated from different places (first the wrist, then the elbow), the thumb hinge works in exactly the same way.

The thumb hinge can work only if the thumb is stationary. Think of the thumb as the fulcrum point for the vibrato motion. We facilitate this by pressing the thumb *lightly* against the neck of the violin, which sets it in its stationary position. With the thumb set, the thumb hinge can move freely.

The position of the thumb is critical here (see Chapter 2). If the thumb is positioned either too high or too low on the neck, the thumb hinge will be prevented from moving. Most important, the thumb *must not* grip the side of the neck. Instead, the thumb provides a light counterpressure to the fingers on the string, while the thumb hinge is kept free and flexible.

Although it is possible to vibrate without moving the thumb hinge, this will not result in an optimal vibrato. The motion of the thumb hinge greatly improves the physical mechanics of vibrato. When the mechanics work well, the vibrato has more variation, which, of course, enhances a violinist's expressive palette.

THE BASIC VIBRATO MOVEMENT

Regardless of the type of vibrato employed (wrist or arm), the basic vibrato movement is the "waving" motion forward and back. There are countless exercises designed to teach the waving motion, from shaking pill bottles to sliding a piece of cloth up and down the string. Many of these exercises have conceptual merit, but transferring the waving motion to a fixed finger on the string can be problematic.

A successful vibrato rests on the ability to keep the muscles of the hand and arm relaxed while at the same time making the waving motion to and fro. This waving motion is *localized at the fingertip* as a rocking movement on the string.

One of the most effective approaches to teaching vibrato is for the teacher to move the student's finger back and forth on the string. This allows the student to feel the vibrato motion at the fingertip, where vibrato is "realized." It also helps the student hear the sound of the vibrato under the ear. Knowing what a good vibrato sounds like can guide the physical effort.

In fact, the waving movement in vibrato is really quite minimal, and a major hurdle for many students is learning how to stay relaxed while making such a fine muscular movement. As mentioned earlier, this is partially a matter of training the muscles, but it also involves learning how to reduce the overall physical effort.

PING

As the basic vibrato movement is established, our next concern is to address the idea of ping. *Ping* is a vivid term that describes the actual sound of the vibrato oscillation. All good vibratos have ping.

The best way to understand the idea of ping is to hear vibrato as a pulse existing *inside* a note. The important quality of ping, or the pulse of the note, is that the pitch of the note does not change with the vibrato. Instead, ping pushes the note forward and out into space, in much the same way a loud-speaker moves the air and displaces the sound. Ping enhances the carrying power of the note.

An example of a vibrato without ping is the overly wide vibrato in which the pitch of the note audibly changes, sometimes by as much as a quarter step. Conversely, a very fast, nervous vibrato can also lack ping because the pulse of the pitch is not audible. A vibrato without ping will sound imposed on the note, whereas a vibrato with ping is integral to the pitch.

The trick to a vibrato with ping lies in the vibrato impulse, or the physical motion of the finger on the string, which is always *forward*. This forward motion is what gives vibrato its energy. The backward movement of the vibrato is passive by comparison, functioning as a rebound. It can be helpful to think of the forward motion as being slightly faster than the backward return. This is more conceptual than anything because in practice the vibrato impulse sounds even.

How much the fingertip moves on the string greatly affects the ping of the vibrato. When we first learn to vibrate, we are often taught to allow the finger to rock back and forth, across the width of the fingertip. Although this is an effective way to first learn the vibrato motion, it produces a wide, slow vibrato that decidedly has no ping.

When working for ping in the vibrato, the rocking movement of the finger on the string is minimized, almost to the point at which it stops altogether. In other words, the vibrato motion becomes localized, encompassing just a small area of the fingertip surface. The effect is that the vibrato becomes focused and ping can be heard.

Here is a simple exercise that helps develop ping:

First, play a note with absolutely no vibrato. Listen to the purity of the pitch.
Now, add the smallest degree of vibrato possible to the pitch while trying to minimize the surface area of the fingertip affected by the vibrato movement.
Go back and forth between no vibrato and the minimum vibrato. See if you can get the vibrato to pulse, or ping, with a minimum of vibrato motion.

In fact, a problem for many violinists is that the vibrato motion is too large, something especially true for players with large hands (like myself). Learning to minimize the vibrato motion can be helpful in this case. However, it is *very* important not to tense the arm while trying to minimize the vibrato movement. Minimizing the motion can actually achieve the opposite of tension — the vibrato becomes more relaxed because the effort is less.

> **Note:**
>
> To develop a vibrato with ping, LESS IS MORE.

Finally, the idea of ping also is closely related to intonation. Ping should enhance rather than distort the purity of the pitch. Nathan Milstein would always say, "intonation before vibrato."

VARIATION — SPEED AND WIDTH

Once ping is developed in the vibrato, a student can begin to vary the vibrato. The ability to vary the vibrato is a powerful tool that allows us to greatly enhance a musical idea. The opposite of a variable vibrato is the automatic vibrato, which always sounds the same, regardless of the music being played. The automatic vibrato tends to detract from the musical expression.

Developing variation in the vibrato depends on two variables: speed and width. In actuality, these two concepts are inextricably linked. To give the vibrato more speed, we usually narrow the width of the vibrato motion. Conversely, to add more width to the vibrato, we tend to slow the speed. The exception to this occurs when we play something very aggressive or very forte. Then, the vibrato tends to increase both in speed and width.

DEVELOPING SPEED

For many players, developing more speed is a problem. In an effort to do so, players often tense the arm muscles in order to make the vibrato motion finer, which is a serious mistake. Just as in the ping exercise, the key to a faster vibrato lies in minimizing the surface area of the fingertip covered by the vibrato motion.

As discussed earlier, this is achieved not by tensing the muscles, but rather by learning to make the vibrato motion smaller. A good vibrato requires training and conditioning of the muscles over time (a violinist out of shape is revealed by a slow vibrato.), but it does *not* include tensing the muscles to achieve the result.

INCREASING WIDTH

Usually, it is easy for students to make the vibrato wider once a faster vibrato has been mastered. Sometimes, however, a student will have a very fast, uncontrolled vibrato and will be unable to slow the vibrato impulse or increase its width. Usually, this type of problem is the result of an overly tense arm vibrato.

It can be a difficult issue to resolve, often requiring relearning vibrato from the ground up. In this case, it is helpful to encourage the student to vibrate more from the wrist.

In the end, the student may still be inclined to vibrate from the arm, but the addition of some wrist movement can help release the problematic muscle tension. The following is an excellent Dounis exercise that can develop the wrist vibrato (Dounis was a strong advocate for wrist vibrato):

Place the second finger on e, fifth position on the G string. The wrist of the left hand will be touching the shoulder of the instrument.
Play e and then shift the finger to f, but make sure the movement is initiated from the wrist.

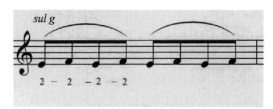

Gradually increase the speed of the shift and make its movement smaller and smaller, until the finger stays on the note e but the wrist continues to move.
Try the movement with the first finger and then the third finger.
As the wrist movement is developed, try the exercise in the third position and finally in the first position.

Where the finger is placed on the string can affect the speed and width of the vibrato. Generally, when playing more on the fingertips, the vibrato will tend to be faster (as the movement covers less surface area). Playing more on the pad of the finger usually results in a wider, or fatter, vibrato. Experimenting with the finger placement can help develop greater variation in the vibrato.

Finally, it is important to keep in mind that ping is the essential ingredient of a good vibrato. As you work for more variation in the vibrato, make sure that ping can still be heard.

SIZZLE

A vibrato's sizzle gives the sound an electric quality. Sizzle occurs when the vibrato speed is slightly faster at the beginning of a note. This often corresponds to the bow's moving faster as well. In Chapter 6, we discussed the idea of attack and release, making the point that all notes have some sort of front, or beginning. Sizzle is very much related to this idea.

An obvious example of sizzle occurs when one plays a series of notes with strong accents. In this case, the bow will move faster for the accent and then slow as the note is sustained. The vibrato should do much the same. The vibrato impulse is fast and wide at the beginning of the note and then narrows and slightly slows as the note is sustained. To facilitate this technique, the finger pressure on the string should release somewhat immediately following the accent.

Sizzle need not be confined to strongly accented notes. In fact, we can and should sizzle on every note vibrated (unless a conscious decision has been made to the contrary, as in using a delayed vibrato or no vibrato). Learning the technique of sizzle goes beyond giving the sound a wonderful buoyancy. It also helps keep the left hand relaxed and light on the string. My teacher, Arthur Grumiaux, was a master of the sizzle technique, as is amply evident in his many recordings.

A good exercise to develop sizzle on all notes is to play the pitches in this passage, first with separate bows and with accents. As you place each finger, imagine that the string produces a quick electric shock causing the finger to "sizzle" at the beginning of the note. After the sizzle, the vibrato slightly slows, narrows, and relaxes. As you continue the exercise, gradually eliminate the accents with the bow (you can begin to slur the notes if you like), but try to maintain the sizzle in the vibrato. The sizzle may lessen in its intensity, as long as it is evident.

Note:

Sizzle is great thing to practice in conjunction with the idea of attack and release. The two techniques really function as one. Together they produce a sound that is vividly alive.

VIBRATING WITH THE "PINKY"

Vibrato with the fourth finger is always difficult at first. Before a student can address this issue, it is important that the vibrato is working fairly well with the first three fingers. In Chapter 3, we discussed the importance of strengthening the little finger. Here, this becomes most important.

Unfortunately, many violinists simply avoid the little finger when it comes to vibrato. They will carefully finger musical passages so that the "pinky" never has to play an expressive note. The "Catch-22" of this approach is that by avoiding the little finger, the player never strengthens it.

Szymon Goldberg, who was a great advocate for developing the fourth finger, would often comment that the fourth finger could produce a particular kind of vibrato, unlike any other finger. This is especially true in the high register of the instrument. There, the fourth finger vibrato impulse can give a note a penetrating focus that the other fingers cannot.

There are no tricks for developing a strong fourth finger vibrato. Vibrating with the pinky is a matter of strength, which is best cultivated by using the finger. With time and perseverance anyone can attain a beautiful vibrato on the fourth finger.

8

ON PRACTICING

Developing physical skills on the violin requires a particular approach to practicing. A good setup is largely a matter of physical training and conditioning — unlike the process of learning a piece of music, in which much of a student's effort lies in mastering notes and rhythms. The speed at which students master these physical skills varies greatly. Some find them relatively easy to achieve; others need more time and the careful observation and encouragement of a teacher. In the end, I believe *all* students can master the basics of violin playing if given the chance.

How can we maximize the success of our practice while working toward a good setup?

THE "BIG PICTURE"

The first step toward mastering the violin setup is to establish in the mind's eye the "big picture." In other words, one must know what good violin playing looks like. This means understanding both the microcosm of violin playing (particulars such as holding the violin, the bow grip, the left hand frame, and so forth) and the macrocosm, or how individual physical components come together to create a totality of form and movement. The material in this book mainly addresses the elements of the microcosm. The macrocosm will be understood mostly through the observation of others playing well.

There are a variety of ways to develop the big picture. Teacher demonstration is, of course, the most valuable of these. The teacher who is able to demonstrate will always achieve superior results. Students also will learn much from watching each other play, particularly in a studio that has a mix of levels. The more advanced students become role models for those younger or less experienced. Master classes, group classes, and studio recitals are all good venues that encourage peer observation.

In this day of digital media, students and teachers now have a wealth of video resources available to them. These are wonderful supplementary materials. Videotapes or DVDs of great violinists such as Heifetz, Oistrakh, Milstein, Szeryng, and Grumiaux, to name but a few, both inspire and help to create the big picture.

Finally, attending live concerts that feature violin soloists should be strongly encouraged. Nothing can quite replace the impact of a live concert.

TEACHING OUR BODIES

Assuming that the big picture has been established in the mind of a player, we can turn our attention to teaching our bodies the forms and movements of playing.

The accomplished violinist relies on a complicated series of automatic muscular movements, the result of years of training. These skills are the result of the mind–body interplay. The proper relationship here is that the mind directs the body. Susan Kempter, in *How Muscles Learn: Teaching the Violin With the Body in Mind,* writes:

> During the early stages of learning, muscle combinations, tensions and releases are under conscious control and continue to change and reconfigure themselves according to what the mind has ordered. In other words, a perceptual mandate creates a mental template. The muscles, through trial and error, attempt to achieve what the mind has conceived, or come as close to the template as possible (Kempter, 2003).

The body is most receptive when a student first learns a new muscular form or movement. In this circumstance, the critical task is to ensure that the mind sends the correct commands to the body. Especially in the case of young children first learning, the teacher's role is to oversee and monitor that process. A student's body at this stage is essentially a blank slate and will readily acquire new forms and movements as directed by the mind, which is why it is vital to "get things right" from the very start.

This process becomes more problematic when a student has incorrectly learned a physical movement and needs to retrain the body. In this case, the mind must first stop the learned, automatic movement and then replace it with a new one that is not automatic at all, but rather under the conscious control of the mind. This extra step requires considerable mental effort. Attempts to retrain the physical movement will be frustrated by the body's tendency to revert to the original learned movement as soon as the mind stops monitoring the physical effort. A teacher working with a student to change a physical form or movement must be able to teach the new information to the student and then help the student stay mentally focused on acquiring the new physical skills.

When learning (or relearning) physical skills, the process always begins with the cognitive, or the mind's command. As the skill is slowly acquired, the next stage is one of refinement, but it is still very much a product of the mind's control. Finally, the body accepts the new movement or form and it becomes automatic and independent of the mind.

BALANCING THE PHYSICAL WITH THE MUSICAL

Let's not forget that violin playing is an artistic endeavor and not an athletic sport. It is true that violin playing is very physical and that great virtuoso performers do exhibit an athletic quality, but we are first and foremost musicians. When working on physical problems, it is important not to lose sight of the art of music making.

With this in mind, teachers must try to balance the physical side of violin playing with musical development. When first introducing new ideas relating to the physical setup, it is a good idea to focus *only* on those issues. It is a mistake to have a student work on difficult repertoire while learning basic physical skills. Remember, a student needs to focus *all* his or her mental effort on training the body when first encountering new physical issues.

The material assigned to the student should be kept to a minimum, so that the entire practice effort is devoted to learning the new skills. Perhaps a single scale and a single easy etude are enough material for a whole week. An assignment of this sort might apply to a student learning to draw a straight bow. In this case, spending an entire week (and maybe even longer) practicing scales, playing open strings, and learning an easy etude of long bows might be appropriate.

As the physical movements begin to solidify, they can gradually be applied to a piece of music. At this stage, keep the music easy but relevant to the problems being addressed. As new ideas are mastered, they can then be tested in a more ambitious work.

TIPS FOR THE PRACTICE ROOM

When a student first begins work on a particular physical problem associated with the violin setup, this can be a time of frustration and tedium. After all, we just want to play. Why does it have to be so difficult?

1. PUT THE CLOCK AWAY

To help alleviate such feelings, it is, first of all, a good idea to put the clock away. How long one practices when first learning new physical movements is the last concern. In fact, a good strategy is to practice in small increments of ten or fifteen minutes. During these mini-sessions, the entire focus should be devoted to the new physical skill being addressed. Since the body learns by repetition, several mini practice sessions during a given day can reap quick results.

In any one mini-session, avoid too many repetitions of an idea. Remember, the mind must direct the work at this stage. As soon as the attention wanders, stop. If several issues are being addressed in the session, spend only a few minutes working on each one and then stop. After a lengthy break, come back and try things again. This method allows the body to absorb the new sensations, and it gives the mind a rest.

Trying to work on problems of this nature in a long, extended practice session is largely a waste of time. Think of babies first learning to walk. They do so in tiny increments that begin tentatively but progressively become stronger until, at last, they can do it.

2. USE A MIRROR

When working on issues related to the setup, a full-length mirror is indispensable. Every violinist should have one. Practicing in front of a mirror allows a player visually to monitor the physical playing. Perhaps the best way to practice with a mirror is to face it so that the scroll of the violin points directly toward the surface of the mirror. From this angle, it is easy to observe the important lines of violin playing for both right and left sides. Keep in mind that a mirror is useful only if the student understands the big picture and keeps it firmly in mind.

3. STAND

Stand when you practice, especially when working on physical issues. Though violinists sit for much of the time, sitting during practice tends to encourage postural laziness, even for players with the best of intentions. The standing position will foster good physical habits, which we can apply to sitting posture.

4. LISTEN TO THE BODY

Finally, listen to the body. If the body is fatigued, it will not respond well to new commands. When muscles tire, stop. Give them time to recover before working on the problem again. Students working on developing the vibrato, for example, will usually feel some muscular fatigue in the forearm, especially when trying to acquire more intensity in the vibrato impulse. This is normal to a point. However, it is important to realize that the muscles involved in the vibrato must be trained over a period of time. Trying to work through the fatigue is a grave mistake, as this will invite injury in the form of tendonitis or some similar malady.

Tightness is a sign of fatigue and strain. If the muscles begin to tighten, stop and wait until they relax again. Sometimes, muscles will feel tight when you are first beginning to practice. In this case, warm up slowly until they loosen. If, after a careful warm-up, they do not loosen, this could be an indication that the muscles have been stressed. If so, take the day off.

On this subject, stretching exercises are especially beneficial for violinists. Yoga, in particular, is a wonderful way to counter the buildup of muscular tension. Any physical exercise will help alleviate the inevitable aches and pains associated with violin playing. Although the muscles perform many minute movements in violin playing, strength and flexibility are still essential.

ATTITUDE IS EVERYTHING

The importance of avoiding anxiety and frustration cannot be overemphasized. Working on physical problems can cause feelings of this sort, often accompanied by a sense of failure as a player. High or over-achievers often fall prey to these feelings. Of course, this frame of mind is counterproductive to learning new things. The body reacts to such feelings negatively, usually in the form of tension or other types of stress.

Cultivating the right mental attitude is extremely important. On this point, I recommend developing the "observer mind." Too often, students evaluate their work emotionally, or subjectively. The observer mind, on the other hand, steps away from the work at hand and views it from a distance in a critical and dispassionate way. The observer mind evaluates the practice session as if some other person were doing the work. The observer mind never personalizes the work. For example, if a particular passage is played badly out of tune, the observer mind will say, "That was terribly out of tune," as opposed to the personalized response, "I'm terrible."

When the observer mind governs the practice, the student will view the work more as a process rather than a goal-oriented venture. This is healthy and might even foster a sense of humor about oneself. Eventually, one might even be able to laugh at the many trials and tribulations of violin playing, which I think is a good way to be.

SELECTED BIBLIOGRAPHY

Fischer, Simon. *Basics.* London: Peters Edition, 1997.

Flesch, Carl. *The Art of Violin Playing.* New York: Carl Fischer, 1924.

Galamian, Ivan. *Principles of Violin Playing and Teaching.* Englewood Cliffs, NJ: Prentice Hall, 1962, 1985.

Kempter, Susan. *How Muscles Learn: Teaching the Violin With the Body in Mind.* Miami: Summy-Birchard Music, 2003.

Leland, Valborg. *The Dounis Principles of Violin Playing.* New York: Joseph Patelson Music House, 1982.

INDEX